Awakening Grassroots Spirituality

A Celtic Guide for Nurturing and Maturing the Soul

Edwin M. Leidel, Jr.

iUniverse, Inc.

New York   Lincoln   Shanghai

Awakening Grassroots Spirituality
A Celtic Guide for Nurturing and Maturing the Soul

iUniverse, Inc.

For information address:
iUniverse, Inc.
2021 Pine Lake Road, Suite 100
Lincoln, NE 68512
www.iuniverse.com

ISBN: 0-595-31627-1

Printed in the United States of America

Contents

Preface

We are coming to the end of a phase in church life. Increasingly, people look for a spirituality that sees life as a journey, and for a church that connects with God in that journey and in the web of life.

Such a change has taken place before. The "one shape fits all" diocesan structures evolved, in Celtic lands, into friendly villages of God that fitted contemporary social patterns. The people's monastic churches fostered a spirituality of prayer-rhythms, soul friendship, pilgrimage, creativity and hospitality that from the fifth century turned Ireland, and later England into a land of saints and scholars.

The clergy did not burn out, and the bishop was freed from organizational work, because at the heart of each region or diocese was the praying community. This was the hearth, at the center of the church in that region. Through the bishops the people retained their unity with the undivided universal church.

This is an overlooked but vital part of our Episcopal/Anglican birthright. If we are to connect with our changing world, which is turning its back on what is second hand, imposed or fragmented; we need to reconnect with these roots.

Since God changed me from a parish to a pilgrim centered priest, earthed in the Community of Aidan and Hilda, I have longed to discover a community that would allow a Celtic experiment to take place.

The peace of the world may hinge upon the emergence in the rich West of a Christian countermovement as significant as were the desert (Eastern) and the Celtic churches of the early centuries. If oppressed Muslim populations realize that there is a form of Christianity that is not prey to the twin idols of greed and power, but is based upon the Beatitudes and is in solidarity with poor as well as rich people, they will see Christians as sisters and brothers.

In this guide, Bishop Ed Leidel shares with us such a vision, and gives us some tools with which to bring the vision into being. The book helps us explore what it might mean to have a hearth—God's hearth—at the heart of a person, a parish, and a diocese.

May God bless it. I hope there will be a wholehearted response.

Ray Simpson
Epiphany 5, 2003
Guardian of the Community of Aidan and Hilda, the Open Gate, Berwick Upon Tweed, UK

How this Guide Came to be

Being the first bishop of a brand new diocese has been an intense joy and challenge to me these past seven years. The people of the Diocese of Eastern Michigan have demonstrated a persistent desire to forge the way ahead as an Anglican community in ways that are different from the past, and in ways that are pregnant with the possibility of renewing some of our tired old ways.

During these past seven years, we have experimented together with our external structures—with our decision making processes and with the economic stewardship of our communal life. We have also worked hard at leadership development and congregational development. We have often failed in realizing our dreams; but our appetites have been whetted enough for us to believe that God is with us and guiding us in this venture.

In 2002, it began to become clear that renewing external structures was not all that God was requiring of us. Our inner—our soul life—also needed a reawakening. The inner "hearth" of our diocesan community needed a rekindling. This became clear as we received the feedback from the congregational health surveys. Our *Natural Church Development* scores consistently showed a need to reawaken our expression of a "passionate spirituality." So the timing of a sabbatical was right on the mark. As bishop, I needed time to shift my leadership from external development to spiritual growth.

Photo by Ira Leidel

So, the Standing Committee's support for a four-month sabbatical gave the opportunity to respond to this need. I have written this "Guide" on spirituality over a seven-day period beginning at St. Deiniol's Gladstone Library in Hawarden, Wales, and at Lauragh, in County Cork, Ireland—an isolated "edge" place on the Beara Peninsula where mountain and water come together. Just previous to those days of writing, my wife and I had a marvelous and magical time of pilgrimage through some of Ireland's and England's other "boundary" places where mighty Celtic and Anglo-Saxon saints lived and left their marks.

This Guide is a work in progress. It is not intended to offer a simplistic formula for soul-journeyers to follow; but rather, it is an incomplete work, offering the reader many opportunities to deepen their own life towards spiritual authenticity and completeness.

I am indebted to so many for having had this opportunity to put in writing what I have wanted to express in an orderly fashion going back almost twenty years ago. I want to thank the people of St. Timothy's in Indianapolis for listening and responding to my first efforts at defining unique spiritual deserts. Meeting John Westerhoff and having the opportunity to read and talk with him encouraged my first explorations into Jungian personality differentiation theory and into the world of the Myers-Briggs Type Inventory. I also want to thank the marvelous people of St. Christopher's Church in St. Paul, Minnesota, where—working with Jay Hanson (a clergy colleague from a neighboring congregation)—we put together our first "Deserts and Wells" workshops for the city of St. Paul, Minnesota congregations and for members of the Minnesota Great Lakes Area Jungian Type community. More recently, the clergy of the Diocese of Eastern Michigan allowed me to share with them an updated rendition of the Desert and Wells retreat which I renamed, "Riding the Whirlwind: Discerning Sacred Journeys in a Transforming Universe." Thanks to all who allowed the ideas of these workshops to filter into your lives. The feedback that I received has contributed to the ideas expressed in this new guide. Most of all I want to thank the clergy and the laity of Eastern Michigan for encouraging my ministry with them. They have been my primary teachers and mentors.

Most of what follows is a reintegration of spiritual wisdom that has been around for a long time. However, the setting side by side of the Jungian mental functions with Eight Spiritual "Deserts and Wells," and connecting those descriptions to the Eight Vices and Virtues of Eastern Orthodoxy has, to my knowledge, not been done by anyone until this writing.

All photographs in this Guide are taken by me, unless otherwise noted.

Ed Leidel
Epiphany 2, 2003
Hawarden, Wales & Lauragh, County Cork, Ireland

Introduction

Grassroots Transformation

Jesus was clearly a grassroots organizer. He began where people were. He cared about the poor and the disenfranchised. He networked twelve fishermen and their families to begin a community based organization that we now call the Christian Church. Jesus opposed the oppressive self-serving structures of Rome and the Temple enterprise in Jerusalem. Most importantly, Jesus told the Truth. He proclaimed a good-news message that reestablished what the Creator intended at the beginning of the world. Jesus proclaimed a vision of a Kingdom where everyone was a citizen of infinite worth; a Kingdom where leaders were servants, and where servants were just as important as leaders. Jesus assured his disciples that God's healing Grace was accessible to everyone.

Grassroots is about being the community of the baptized, where every member of the baptized is essential to the well being of the community, and where every member is regarded with equal respect.

The American Heritage Dictionary defines grassroots as "the groundwork or source of something." Perhaps what gives grassroots its greatest meaning in our Christ-centered community is the notion that God's Grace is the source (grass-roots) of our ministry. Without God's Grace and Presence all we do is pointless.

St. Brigit, one of the earliest and most popular of the Celtic saints, identified with all classes as equals, though she herself was of royal heritage. Her love for the poor and disenfranchised became legendary. Brigit lived intuitively and naturally in God's presence.

In her desire to give a sign of God's love to anyone who desired it she invented a cross of grass which could be simply made by every person. Brigit's cross of grass (or reeds) has become a Celtic symbol of God's presence with ordinary people. Brigit, Patroness of Ireland, is one of the great icons of grassroots spirituality.

This guide is about grassroots spirituality; it's about a spirituality that is accessible to everyone; it's about growing in God's Presence in community.

Awakening Passion

In the 1990 movie, *Awakenings*, a pioneering neurologist Malcolm (Robin Williams) uses an experimental drug to "awaken" patients from their pseudo-catatonic state in a ward that is called "the garden" where previous treatment has been limited to simply "watering and feeding" the patients. The patients make remarkable recoveries. A one time pianist plays the piano again. All are in awe of being alive again, after years of lost consciousness. The doctor's first patient, Leonard (Robert De Niro) leaves the "garden" and soon embraces everything around him, and wants to experience more and more of life. Tragically, the medication's effects wane, and all of the patients give in to the inevitability of returning to their previous catatonic existences.

Awakenings is based on the real life experiences of its neurologist author, Dr. Oliver Sacks. In his book *Awakening* (on which the movie is based) and in many other works, Sacks gives evidence of the extraordinary capacities of human beings who emerge from cases of disability or breakdown. He shows human consciousness to be something altogether vaster and more wonderful than dreamt of in our worldly philosophies. In his 1982 book, *A Leg to Stand On*, Sacks recalls how his "dead" leg, severed in a mountaineering accident and sewn back on, miraculously comes back to life when he listens to a taped concert of a Mendelssohn violin concerto.

Sack's observations remind us that there is much in life that remains marvelously open and unexplored. This becomes especially evident as we become aware of how trapped and blind-sighted our soul-consciousness has become living in a time that takes such pleasure in demythologizing mystery and miraculous expectation. But times are changing. There are signs all around us of a yearning and hunger for guidance in living a life more fully open to the wonder of God's awesome Passion and Presence. The fact that you are reading these words gives evidence to this need.

Spirituality is about Relationship

Love is about relationship. The experience of passion is relational. Our life with God begins relationally with the heart. Spirituality is about being in a right relationship with the Living God who we experience personally as Source, Brother, and Breath. Awakening to God begins with awakening the experiences of relationships.

The Scriptures deal with discerning call in three categories: (1) right relationship, (2) right belief, and (3) right behavior. Anglicans, with our roots in Celtic and Eastern Orthodox spirituality, have tended to put these three sources of truth into a procedural order, beginning incarnationally with **right relationship** in community; then proceeding to discern **right belief** from within the conversation of Christian community; and then proceeding finally to come to grasps with **right behavior** and the appropriate habits of the heart to encourage right behavior.

Western Christianity (after the Council of Whitby in 664) has tended to change this procedural order for discerning truth, beginning rather with (1) right belief (based axiomatically upon Scripture, Tradition, and hierarchal encyclicals: all of which begin to take on a kind of authority defined by a church leadership that cannot be questioned or put over against life experience); then one proceeds to (2) right behavior which follows automatically from right belief and which is mandated by detailed doctrinal definitions; and then finally one graduates to (3) right relationship which can often, but not necessarily, take on a "we true believers are better then you" attitude.

The sixteenth century Reformation attempted to correct the problematic expressions of this way of doing moral theology by giving authority back to the laity. Unfortunately, the Western priority of Law before community remained. It seems to me that today we are attempting to complete the work of the Reformation—which in my mind would restore the process of doing moral theology to the ancient, challenging, and highly responsible Celtic way that begins with community, progresses to commitment, and ends with conversion.

Jesus echoed what the Old Testament taught, which was to Love God with all of your heart, soul, mind and strength, and to Love your neighbor as yourself. He said this was the summary of the Law, and that there was no greater commandment than this. Right relationship is about being in a right and loving relationship with our Creator and all of God's creation. That's the beginning of our spiritual pilgrimage. It is then, within the context of a loving and accepting community, that we (no matter who or what we are) experience the amazing Grace of God. We then begin to yearn to have a right belief, a right view of creation and human nature that fits the Love that we are experiencing. That right belief is conditioned by Scripture (the past experience of the people of God) as well as by current experiences of God's Love which test, ratify, magnify and flesh out the ancient truths of Scripture. And so we enter into an ongoing journey of transformation, going as St. Paul says from "glory to glory."

Celtic Spirituality:
An ancient Tradition as a Contemporary Resource

Robert Cahill's popular, *How the Irish Saved Civilization* (1995), opened the minds of many of us to the often forgotten contributions that the Irish culture of the 5th through 10th centuries—a culture which was totally Celtic and Christian—made to the preservation, and to some of the uniqueness of today's western culture. In 664 AD a historic church synod was held at Whitby in Northumbria (on the west coast of England) at which the ways of the powerful, wealthy, and structured Church of Rome were judged to be superior to the troublesomely spreading ways of the "provincial and remote" English and Irish. 664 is often referred to as that time when the western church began to favor a "St. Peter" type of spiritual ethos, emphasizing the "head," institutional structure, and rational order; over a "St. John" type of spiritual ethos, emphasizing the "heart," simplicity of life, and organic (creation centered) community. This comparison and its reference to a definitive date is a great over-simplification of history. However, the setting side by side of these two strands of Christian spirituality resonates with our present experience that the church has become "out of balance." For many of us, the church has become an overly institutional structure which seems to lack a spirituality that has the passion and context to challenge today's growing darkness and complexities.

Celtic scholar Ray Simpson observes that Western Protestantism has tended to separate Christ out of the Trinity, making it difficult for today's growing numbers of Islamic people to comprehend and value our experience of God as a singular Being, manifest to us in a Trinity of Persons.[1] David Adam, one of today's best known advocates of the Celtic Way, reminds us that a fully Trinitarian theology must include the Celtic awareness of God incarnately present in all of creation:

[In St. Ninian] we find a desire to discover the presence of God in all of things, something that modern Christians seem to fear. Because of the fear of pantheism, many Christians seem to have banned God form his creation. A friend of mine who is a bishop says, "I do not like saying, "The Lord is here" within a service.' This brought from me the response, 'If God is not here, then where is he?' The bishop, being a deep thinker, was instant in his reply, 'I do not want to give the impression that God is only in church.' So my final comment on the matter was, 'Well then, go around the supermarkets, the railway stations, the factories and declare "God is here" by your presence, your care, your self-giving.'…One of the great gifts from the Celtic Church to us is in the emphasis on the presence of God at all times and in all things [the animals, birds, fishes, forests, plants]. There is no separation of the sacred and secular, into body and soul, into heaven and earth. All are one in God. There is nothing outside of God or his love. It is only our blindness that prevents us from seeing the glory that is in all things.[2]

There is much in Celtic religion of the first millennium of the church that is clearly applicable and retrievable for a revitalized and reformed church of the third millennium. We need a spirituality today that is:

1. Earth-conscious and environmentally concerned.
2. Includes and values the poorest of the poor, and all of the outcasts of a power and money hungry world. A spirituality that is inclusive of all people.
3. Balanced between its concerns for institutional order and its concern for communal care.
4. Balanced between its use of head, heart, soul, and body.
5. Aware of God's presence in, as well as above, and beyond all of creation.
6. Truly passionate in its love of God, and of God's creation.
7. Disciplined and willing to give its life away for the sake of the world, following the example of Jesus.
8. Filled with the wildness and wonder of the mystery and awe in life.
9. Values creativity and imagination as dimensions of the Divine life within the human spirit.
10. "Grassroots" and organic in its way of making decisions and organizing its life.

This Guide is an attempt to recapture and apply a passionate and "Celtic-like" spirituality that will help individuals, small groups and dioceses to live productively and joyfully in the challenging days ahead.

Most of the nine sections of the Guide stand on their own and can be used as a personal or group study without reference to sections that come before it. However, sections five and six are the most challenging, and will be more useful after reading the sections that come before.

Section Summaries

Section One
Tears in the Wilderness

This section proposes a starting place for a deeper journey into the depths of one's soul life. It is suggested that an awareness of personal and worldly brokenness must be the catalyst that energizes a fresh start. This is not a new idea. The scriptures and the lives of the saints document this need. Remorse, tears, contrition and confession are good for the soul. The fifties through the nineties urged us to work at gaining self respect. However, real self respect is grounded in honest humility and an awareness of our personal and corporate "dark" sides. Spiritual growth is only possible as we confront the demons that lurk within and without.

Section Two
The Longing for Healthy Community

Yearning for utopia is a part of the human condition. Something within tells us that the communities in which we are formed are never quite all that they might be. At this time in history when our social order is in disarray and seeking reformation, we are experiencing a particularly strong "hunger and thirst" for healthy community. The hippy experiments of the sixties were a juvenile beginning of this longing. Once again as we enter the new millennium, there are new experiments of communal living being initiated that have a more mature and Christian character. Many of these new Christian "hearths" have a decidedly Celtic personality.

Section Three
Searching for an Integrated Lifestyle:
Breathing In and Breathing Out

There are few who would disagree with the judgment that our lives today feel "out of control." What, we wonder, can anchor our anxieties and steer us on a course from which the slightest little breeze will not disorient us? When we dare to analyze our use of time and wealth, we inevitably discover serious imbalances. We know that something is not right, but we seem incapable of changing our course. Celtic spirituality as evidenced in fifth through tenth century Ireland, Wales, Scotland and England (while not utopian) did provide a balanced way of living. Life in those days, like today, was chaotic, hard and challenging. Yet the Christian Church thrived. Perhaps our Celtic ancestors have something from which we can learn.

Section Four
Four Gateways to Pastures of the Soul

All souls do not look or behave alike. Ancient monastic communities, as well as Christian denominations have all taken on personalities of their own. These institutional formations were all creations of particular historical contexts. The past has produced a wealth of spiritualities from which we may choose.[3] Each of us tends to find more affinity and comfort in a particular Christian tradition or spirituality. In the twentieth century Carl Jung and others demonstrated that we are all created genetically unique; and yet within our peculiar differences there are patterns of similarity. In fact there are four wonderfully unique spiritualities which have very different characteristics. This section seeks to describe those four different pastures for the soul, and to invite the reader into the pasture that best harvests the Divine Presence for their soul's deepest hungers.

Section Five
Eight Deserts and Wells of Grace:
Towards Developing a Phenomenology for Soul Life

This section continues the journey into particular terrains of the soul, demonstrating that different souls experience different tendencies to destruction and dis-ease, as well as different tendencies to recovery and growth. Each of the four spiritualities of the previous section is further refined to two sub-spiritualities or soul types with their own deserts and wells of Grace. The different desert and wells characteristics of some of the Church's great mystics and saints are briefly discussed. The stages of the soul's journey into the desert, and out again, are described. A connection is made between the classical vices and virtues, and eight spiritualities of the soul. Readers are invited to chart their own soul's journey into the desert, and to name there the wells of grace that they encounter.

Section Six
The Three Conversions:
Necessary Pilgrimages for the Soul-Journeyer

The formation and maturity of the soul is a life-long process. It is a journey of three significant conversions. God has ingeniously given to the Church special moments on the journey when our communities of faith give to us new opportunities for moving on down the road. Baptism, Confirmation and Holy Communion are opportunities for discovering who we are, why we are, and what is that we must do. Baptism is about identity—it is about who we are. Confirmation is about vocation—what it is that we must do. And Holy Communion is about molding our life into a Christ like life, where like Jesus, we give our life away for the sake of the world. Baptism, Confirmation and Holy Communion are not just "once, and that's it" experiences. Our need to discover who we are, what we are for, and what we must die for—all relate with one another. We regularly renew our baptismal vows, we change jobs, and we re-envision what it is that ultimately is to be our life's work. This section invites soul journeyers into an examination of their gifts, of their call, and of their ultimate destiny.

Section Seven
Developing Habits of the Heart for Living
in the Presence of God

The soul journeyer, like any traveler needs a map, a suitcase, and soul friends if they are to make any progress on their journey. This section explores the need for spiritual disciplines to keep one on course, as well as the kinds of tools that our suitcases need to carry to keep us healthy. We often fail in our desire to grow spiritually because we have not properly equipped ourselves for the long haul. There are time proven aids that give direction and endurance to the soul as it seeks union with God, and fulfillment in the world. Soul journeyers must design their own habits of the heart or rule of life, because every soul journeyer is unique.

Section Eight
Visioning a "Village of Heaven"
for Today's Future Church

When Celtic author Ray Simpson first reviewed this Guide, he said that he would like to see this section further up front, as he thought it was the most important section. I mention that here for those who might want to start their study with this section. I have put this section at the end because it is the most unfinished of all the sections, and because it invites the reader to write the final sentences for themselves, by the way they chose to live their lives in the future. Clearly, God is calling us to reform and return to a way of being the Church that will breath new life into our lives and that will maintain that new life in a world that has substantially changed. There is much evidence to propose that this new life should have a character similar to that of ancient Celtic Christianity. Cell life may well be the source of the future church's soul life. What would a diocese look like that restructured itself into hearth centers that were intentionally designed to grow and nurture healthy souls for the purpose of experiencing God, and for the purpose of reconciling our broken world?

Section Nine
Conclusion:
Encouragements for Beginning Again

The concluding section begins with a summary of the purpose and flow of this guide for awakening soul life. Soul journeying in the context of creation's many cycles is considered. Finally three encouragements for beginning the journey again are offered: joy, trust and paying attention.

Section One

Tears in the Wilderness

A voice cries in the wilderness,
Prepare the way of the Lord;
Clear a straight path for him.

John the Baptist appeared in the wilderness proclaiming a baptism
in token of repentance, for the forgiveness of sins; and everyone
flocked to him from the countryside of Judea and the city of
Jerusalem, and they were baptized by him in the River Jordon
confessing their sins.

—Mark 1: 3-5

This is John the Baptist's response to a culture out of balance, and on its way towards self-destruction. Jesus' response to cousin John is dramatic. Accepting John's appraisal of the world's disorder, Jesus receives the baptism of *metanoia* and goes off to the wilderness for 40 days seeking his Father's vocation for him to confront and heal the world's brokenness.

In December of 2002 and January of 2003 my wife and I undertook a sixty-five day sabbatical pilgrimage which took us from Glendalough in Ireland to Lindisfarne and Whitby in Northumbria in the UK to the Dingle Peninsula of County Kerry back in Ireland—all "thin places" (Celtic term for places where the boundaries between heaven and earth are indistinguishable) of holy Celtic origins. I interviewed a number of prophetic leaders, who like John the Baptist, are trying to discern a new way into God's future for the earth; to repent of the past, and risk new prophetic forms of community for the future. I also had the sabbatical joy of gleaning treasures from some fifty volumes of spirituality, history and prose. I write now of this experience which I firmly believe has been Spirit led and which will significantly influence my days ahead.

Where do I begin? The desert was where the heroes and heroines of Irish monasticism began in the fourth century. It is where the Baptist and Jesus began, following the example of Moses and the forty years of Israel's pilgrimage through the Sinai desert. The desert, a place of emptying, is where I must begin.

The desert is both personal and global. The desert is a place of nakedness where all superficiality is stripped away. It is a place of honest revelation. So let me be honest. On a personal level, I confess and repent of my very real incompetence and of my unworthiness (sinner that I am) to be in a calling of discipleship and leadership in God's Holy Church. My inability to live a fully disciplined life of prayer and generosity with others weighs heavy on my soul. I have not trusted fully in the gifts that God has given to me, and I have squandered too many opportunities to effect reconciliation and justice. I eat too much and I do not exercise enough. I spend and hoard too much. I fail often at being a good husband and father. I have paid far too much attention to the causes of worldly success and institutional survival.

I Am Not Worthy

Early in my years as a parish priest, I had a simple picture hanging in my office of a penitent bent over in prayer, saying "Father forgive me, I am not worthy." I do not know what has happened to that "icon" of truth. I miss the Prayer of Humble Access, where we would confess that "we are not worthy:"

We do not presume to come to this thy Table, O merciful Lord, trusting in our own righteousness, but in thy manifold and great mercies. We are not worthy so much as to gather up the crumbs under thy Table. But thou art the same Lord whose property is always to have mercy. Grant us therefore, gracious Lord, so to eat the flesh of thy dear Son Jesus Christ, and to drink his blood, that we may evermore dwell in him, and he in us. *Amen.* (Book of Common Prayer, p.337)

Our liturgical revisions of the 1970's were greatly needed and have served the church well; but as is often the case in reforming movements, we may have thrown out "the baby with the bath water." It was good to see a form of the humble access prayer come alive again in the current liturgies in England, Wales and Ireland that I experienced on our sabbatical travels.

At St. Christopher's, in St. Paul, Minnesota I had the privilege of knowing Russ Lucas, a popular and much loved pediatric cardiologist who often began public addresses by introducing himself as "a miserable sinner." Russ was truly a healer of hearts and souls.

Russ's words mirror the attitude and perspective of the saints of the past. Note the straight forward and honest humility of St. Patrick, one of the first and best known of the Celtic saints:

I am Patrick, a sinner, most unlearned, the least of all the faithful, and utterly despised by many…. But of what help is an excuse, however true, especially if combined with presumption, since now, in my old age, I strive for something that I did not acquire in youth? It was my sins that prevented me from fixing in my mind what before I had barely read through…. And He inspired me—me, the outcast of this world—before others, to be the man (if only I could!) who, with fear and reverence and without blame, should faithfully serve the people to whom the love of Christ conveyed and gave me for the duration of my life, if I should be worthy; yes indeed, to serve them humbly and sincerely…. Hence I ought unceasingly to give thanks to God who often pardoned my folly and my carelessness, and on more than one occasion spared His great wrath on me, who was chosen to be His helper and who was slow to do as was shown me and as the Spirit suggested…. I pray those who believe and fear God, whosoever deigns to look at or receive this writing which Patrick, a sinner, unlearned, has composed in Ireland, that no one should ever say that it was my ignorance if I did or showed forth anything however small according to God's good pleasure; but let this be your conclusion and let it so be thought, that—as is the perfect truth—it was the gift of God. This is my confession before I die.[4]

When Jesus sent the Twelve out for the first time, he sent them out on a mission of repentance and healing:

> As he went about the villages teaching, he summoned the Twelve and sent them out two by two with authority over unclean spirits…. So they set out and *proclaimed the need for repentance*; they drove out many demons, and anointed many sick people with oil and cured them."
>
> —Mark 6: 6b-13

In 1936, Evelyn Underhill put it all so well in a series she did on BBC radio, now in book form simply called *The Spiritual Life*:

> "We spend most of our time conjugating three verbs: to Want, to Have and to Do. Craving, clutching, and fussing on the material, political, social, emotional, intellectual—even on the religious—plane, we are kept in perpetual unrest: forgetting that none of these verbs have any ultimate significance, except so far as they are transcended by and included in the fundamental verb, to Be: and that Being, not wanting, having and doing, is the essence of a spiritual life…. The people of our time are helpless, distracted and rebellious, unable to interpret that which is happening, and full of apprehension about that which is to come, largely because they have lost this sure hold on the eternal; which gives to each life meaning and direction….[5]

My experience of desert and sin is more than personal; it is also global. I am part of a global community that seems stuck in its inability to come to terms with war, violence, hunger, disease, justice for all, racism, and environmental degradation. Many have been the times when I have felt frustrated by a local congregation's unwillingness to even admit the realities of the world's present darkness. Not enough have been the nights when I have wet my pillow with tears for the plight of God's island earth.

Alan Jones has a chapter on "The Gift of Tears" in his excellent book, <u>Soul Making</u>,[6] where he recalls Celia's conversation in T.S. Eliot's <u>The Cocktail Party</u>. Celia says:

> "It's not the feeling of anything I've ever done, which I might get away from, or of anything in me I might get rid of—but of emptiness,

of failure toward someone, or something, outside of myself; and I feel I must atone—is that the right word?"

Jones responds to the question:

"Atone is the word, if the world is to be mended. Weeping is an essential beginning to this atoning work because, without tears, the ego might run in a frenzy of atoning zeal and harm itself and others in the process. Attempts to do some atoning on our own can do great damage by fostering attitudes of righteous rigorism. The gift of tears will have nothing to do with either abject fear or compulsive behavior.... *Penthos* (from the same root as *pathos*, suffering) is often the translation for mourning. Its direct opposite is *accedie*, a lazy sullenness that often masquerades as sorrow, but actually dries up the source of tears. The fruit of true *penthos* is joy and gratitude. The fruit of *accedie* is self-centered morbidity. It hardens the heart, and this hardness must be softened by tears. Evagrius of Ponticus, one of the early desert believers, wrote: 'First pray for the gift of tears, to soften by compunction the inherent hardness of your soul.' For the desert believers, these tears are capable of raising the penitent from his deadness and deadliness. They are tears of a kind of baptism, and therefore, agents of resurrection. Tears act as a medicine that restores the disfigured soul to its true likeness."[7]

And so it is that Jesus proclaims that those who are truly happy are those who weep and mourn (Matthew 5:4). Unhappiness comes to those with dry eyes and cold hearts. Repentance and tears come at that moment when the truth about our self and God strikes home, piercing our heart, and making new life possible again.

In <u>Anam Cara: A Book of Celtic Wisdom</u>, John O'Donohue recalls a wonderful poem by Norman MacCraig which speaks of our ever present need for forgiveness and Grace:

Presents
I give you an emptiness,
I give you a plentitude,
unwrap them carefully.
-one's as fragile as the other-
and when you thank me
I'll pretend not to notice the doubt in your voice
When you say that they're just what you wanted.

Put them on the table by your bed.
When you wake in the mourning
They'll have gone through the door of sleep
into your head. Wherever you go
they'll go with you and
wherever you are you'll wonder,
smiling about the fullness
you can't add to, and the emptiness
you can't fill.

True fullness and presence come in the context of absence and tears. To ignore our need for repentance and block our awareness of desert times is to barricade the soul from its need to journey on. The rhythm of tears and joy, absence and presence, repentance and forgiveness is the necessary stuff of the spiritual life. God's Grace keeps the dialectic going. We are surprised by Grace, accept it and journey on, absorbed in God's embrace.

Repentance and Tears

Ray Simpson came to the Island of Lindisfarne just before Christmas in 1987 empty and seeking God's healing and revealing Presence. The Holy Island is at its most dismal state at this time of year; dark, cold, depopulated—except for those who have come to drink during the holidays. On New Year's Eve he found himself praying in the dark cold of an Island manger-barn. It is there that he experienced the gift of tears and a call to begin the community of Aidan and Hilda.

My wife, Ira and I arrived at Lindisfarne almost 15 years to the date of Ray's experience of Grace in the desert of the Island's dismal winter. On the Island, after listening to Ray tell his story, I recalled how some 15 years earlier, I too had experienced the gift of tears during a time of heritage on the "holy" mountain of the University of the South in Sewanee, Tennessee. For three summers I lived more or less as a hermit in a vacated faculty home for a three week period during a five week time of study, as I worked on a Doctor of Ministry degree. I too was hungry and thirsty for a new sense of identity and purpose in my life, feeling somehow blocked from ever reaching that which was never quite clear. One evening I was unexpectedly overwhelmed with tears with such a force that I ended up buckled over sobbing uncontrollably. And then just as suddenly I experienced a light in the room and a sense of peace deeper than I had ever known.

Repentance and tears mark the beginning of a re-awakening of the Spirit in our lives. Repentance and tears are the gateways that every kind and condition of

Christian pilgrim must go through to continue becoming what God calls them to be. Our remorse must be both personal and corporate. In 1997 pilgrims that were Anglican, Roman Catholic and Reformed journeyed together to the Isle of Lindisfarne where they prayed the following prayer of confession. The prayer realistically captures a corporate sense of the sinfulness that overshadows the church today:

> We confess with shame
> The loss in the church of integrity, humility and patience
> The crushing of spontaneity
> The caging of the wild Spirit
> The breaking off of relationships
> The bruising of the crushed reeds
> The arrogance of the intellect
> The pride of empire-building,
> We accept our share of responsibility for these sins,
> And seek to shed them on behalf of ourselves and our churches.
> Lord, have mercy upon us and forgive us.[8]

I have always found the Liturgy for Ash Wednesday in the Episcopal Book of Common Prayer, to be an intensely moving time of personal and corporate repentance. The "we" language in the Litany of Penitence demonstrates how we can continue to confess our corporate sins:

> Most holy and merciful Father:
> We confess to you and to one another, and to the whole communion of saints in heaven and on earth, that we have sinned by our own fault in thought, word, and deed; by what we have done, and by what we have left undone.
> We have not loved you with our whole heart, and mind, and strength. We have not loved our neighbors as ourselves. We have not forgiven others, as we have been forgiven.
> *Have mercy on us, Lord.*
> We have been deaf to your call to serve, as Christ served us. We have not been true to the mind of Christ. We have grieved your Holy Spirit.
> *Have mercy on us, Lord.*
> We confess to you, Lord, all our past unfaithfulness: the pride, hypocrisy, and impatience of our lives,
> *We confess to you, Lord.*

Our self-indulgent appetites and ways, and our exploitation of other people,
We confess to you, Lord.
Our anger at our own frustration, and our envy of those more fortunate than ourselves,
We confess to you, Lord.
Our intemperate love of worldly goods and comforts, and our dishonesty in daily life and work,
We confess to you, Lord.
Our negligence in prayer and worship, and our failure to commend the faith that is in us,
We confess to you, Lord.
Accept our repentance, Lord, for the wrongs we have done: for our blindness to human need and suffering, and our indifference to injustice and cruelty,
Accept our repentance, Lord.
For all false judgments, for uncharitable thoughts toward our neighbors, and for our prejudice and contempt toward those who differ from us,
Accept our repentance, Lord.
For our waste and pollution of your creation, and our lack of concern for those who come after us,
Accept our repentance, Lord.
Restore us, good Lord, and let your anger depart from us;
Favorably hear us, for your mercy is great.
Accomplish in us the work of your salvation,
That we may show forth your glory in the world.
By the cross and passion of your Son our Lord,
Bring us with all your saints to the joy of his resurrection.

The Bishop, if present, or the Priest, stands and, facing the people, says

Almighty God, the Father of our Lord Jesus Christ, who desires not the death of sinners, but rather that they may turn from their wickedness and live, has given power and commandment to his ministers to declare and pronounce to his people, being penitent, the absolution and remission of their sins. He pardons and absolves all those who truly repent, and with sincere hearts believe his holy Gospel. Therefore we beseech him to grant us true repentance and his Holy Spirit, that those things may please him which we do on this day, and that the rest of our life hereafter may be pure and holy, so that at the last we may come to his eternal joy; through Jesus Christ our Lord. *Amen.*[9]

Exercises:

1. Fredrick Buechner defined "tears" in the following way:

    "You never know what may cause them. The sight of the
    Atlantic Ocean can do it, or a piece of music, or a face you've never
    seen before. A pair of somebody's old shoes can do it. Almost any
    movie made before the great sadness that came over the world after
    the Second World War, a horse cantering across a meadow, the high
    school basketball team running out onto the gym floor at the start
    of a game. You can never be sure. But of this you can be sure.
    Whenever you find tears in your eyes, especially unexpected tears, it
    is well to pay closest attention.

    They are not only telling you something about the secret of who
    you are, but more often than not God is speaking to you through
    them the mystery of where you have come from and is summoning
    you to where, if your soul is to be saved, you should go to next."[10]

    Recall the last time you were surprised by your tears. What might have God
    been saying to you through your tears? What might God have been leading
    you to do next?

2. Pray the following prayer, spending time reflecting on each of its petitions:

    Jesus, you were driven to the sands by the searching Spirit

    Strip from us what is not of you

    Forgive us for our selfish deeds, our empty speech and words with
    which we wound

    Forgive us for our false desires, our vengeful attitudes and for what
    we have left unattended.[11]

3. Spend quiet time remembering what expectations you believed God had for
    you when you first took seriously your decision to become a Christian. How
    many of those expectations are being realized in your life today? How many
    have you forgotten about? Pick out one forgotten aspiration, and formulate
    a plan to recover it back into your life's journey.

4.   Read over the two forms for "The Reconciliation of a Penitent" in the Episcopal <u>Book of Common Prayer</u>, pp. 447-452. Make a list of your most significant sins of commission and omission. Offer up your sins to God in prayer. Some may find useful Martin L. Smith's, <u>Reconciliation: Preparing for Confession in the Episcopal Church</u>.

5.   Make an appointment with a priest to make your sacramental confession, *or* share your list (in 3. above) with a trusted confidant and discuss what new course of action will help you to make amends with the past.

Section Two

Longing for Healthy Community

As a deer longs for flowing streams, so my soul longs for you, O God. My soul thirsts for God, for the living God. When shall I come and behold the face of God?
My tears have been my food day and night, while people say to me continually, "Where is your God?"

—Psalm 42: 1-3

Ever since I can remember I have longed to find and live in a community that would adequately feed and nurture my hunger for affirmation, challenge, honesty, colleagueship, academic stimulation, stewardship, meaningful mission, and communal worship. Whereas my privileged positions as curate, chaplain, rector, dean and bishop within the context of Christian communities have gifted me with abundant graces for which I remain deeply thankful and humbled, my hunger for what Ian Bradley calls a "colony of heaven," lingers on. My wife Ira and I have experimented over the last forty years in Christian communal living in (1) charismatically based communities, (2) parish cell groups and (3) communities intent on renewal and social justice. All of these have been richly rewarding, while also intensely frustrating experiences. Deep within, I know that a perfect community is not realizable in this life. And yet, there seems to be missing in this uncertain age of ours the will for and the components for a truly healthy religious community, whose doors would be open to any whose hunger and thirst would draw them in.

Jerry Doherty, a colleague and Episcopal priest, suggests that the Church's failure today is directly linked to its loss of a continuous, living experience of community. He suggests that we have sold out to an "individualistic" mindset from our culture that has shut us up in the solitude of our own hearts.

> "The Church has been unable to do the mission of becoming the Body of Christ in the world because it has been affected by and become part of the individualistic culture of today...."
>
> "In a society where the Church is trying to respond to individualism we need more community. The Church so far has responded by using short-term events to form temporary communities hoping that the shared feelings will stick when people get home. Camps, retreats, weekend events are examples of programs that can draw people into a community feeling in just a few days. Problems surface after these events when the participants get home to their local parish and find no real community activity there and get depressed and discouraged. They may become an exclusive group to the extent that break away entirely from the whole body and begin meeting on their own. It takes only a few experiences of people expecting instant community in programs to realize that the only lasting community is long-term community in daily living."[12]

Community is larger than we are, precious, impossible to grasp

"The Church desperately needs to become the community it is meant to be. The formation of community in our congregations should be our main task. It is the only way, in my opinion, we can change our fragmented culture…. It is God that people need in their lives. It is an absence of spirituality, the feeling of the presence of God, which has brought our society to the brink of destruction. If we can become God's true community, the Church, we can change the world. This is a great challenge I believe only the churches can meet."

"We must admit that the vast majority of our church congregations are not really communities at all but are doing a more or less good job of faking it."

"The notion that a person or group of people must control everyone else is not community but what is commonly referred to as 'co-depend-ency.' It is a dysfunctional, addictive aggression of people afraid to say what they are thinking or reveal their emotions. Unhappily, it is the way many of our churches function."

"Only by freely admitting un-health can the Church become healthy again."[13]

The work of German theologian, Christian Schwarz these past ten years has produced a list of eight health ingredients[14] that would hypothetically, when fully realized, produce a Christian community that might satisfy the spiritual needs of today's searching pilgrims, and would also, by God's grace, empower the community to fulfill the gospel mandate to redeem the world's brokenness. Schwarz's "Natural Church Development (NCD)"[15] is being tested today by Christians of numerous denominations on all continents. I am impressed by the potential of this creative resource, which we have begun to utilize in the Diocese of Eastern Michigan.

As I listen to other leaders who are using this tool to rekindle healthy community, I have discovered that "passionate spirituality" is the characteristic least present in North American congregations. In Schwarz's scheme, passionate spirituality is defined as

"spiritual intimacy that leads to a strong conviction that God will act in powerful ways. Passionate spirituality is about living the life of faith in a genuine relationship with Jesus Christ."

In the Diocese of Eastern Michigan, 17 of the 35 congregations that are uti-lizing NCD have discovered that this one factor is the most lacking. No other characteristic is so conspicuously absent. From this discovery, one might con-clude that one of the best strategies for regaining healthy Christian community would be closely tied to encouraging and nurturing a passionate Christian spiri-tuality. It is with that idea in mind that I have taken on the work of my sabbatical and of this Guide.[16]

Monasticism seems to have a particularly important role in history during those times when the world and the church are in crisis. "The idea that such [monastic] communities represent a 'leaven within the lump' which is somehow able to revive and stimulate the larger organization is familiar to theologians, his-torians and sociologists alike."[17] The earliest creators of the monastic tradition in the 4th through 6th centuries "represented a movement of more general radical reform which demanded of all Christians fullest adherence to the evangelical-apostolic way of life."[18] The church was of course instituted as an alternative Way of living in the world—a Way designed to bring reconciliation and healing to the self-serving world orders that have always inevitably become dehumanizing and destructive to God's natural order. Whenever the church's institutions have ceased to nurture the culture and overcome its destructive tendencies, experiments in community have risen to initiate new islands of hope to preserve the best of the past and to formulate new ways to live into the future. This seems to have been especially true in the formative years of western monasticism (fourth through eleventh centuries).

Today, as traditional congregations seem less and less attractive to a multi-media bred, earth-sensitive culture, I am aware of a good number of loose knit Christian communities, based on monastic-like spiritual rules that are beginning to spring up in North America, Europe, and Australia.[19] Just type in the words, "spiritual community" or "retreat center" on an internet search engine, and you will find endless lists of alterative Christian (and other) communities. Celtic scholar Ian Bradley asks the question,

"How do we begin to keep in time with the deep pulsations of Eternity and establish colonies of heaven in a society that is profoundly earthborn, materialistic and secular? One way is by establishing com-munities which embrace many of the disciplines of monasticism and have a resident group at their core, but which attract substantial num-bers of adherents who do not practice communal living…. Could it be that in the post-modern, pick-and-choose spiritual supermarket we now inhabit, people are actually craving commitment, discipline and obedience?…Maybe in our dumbed down and easy going culture

Christians should be both proclaiming and living out the essentially counter-culture message of commitment and discipline which is so clearly found in the Celtic and Anglo-Saxon *monastarium.*"[20]

Celtic Spirituality and Community

Jerry Doherty believes that the Celts can teach us a great deal about rebuilding authentic community in today's church.

"The Celtic Christians formed their communities successfully by living a rule of life, by being a spiritual center, a learning center and a community center, which often included training people for ordained ministry for the larger community. They believed that God was present in such community and they fostered a sense and belief in sacred space, especially where true community existed. They can be a model for us as we strive to become church communities in our time that are filled with God's presence and Spirit."

"We cannot make our churches like Celtic communities exclusively. We cannot make broad assumptions that Celtic Christians thought like we do; they did not, but we can look to them for ideas and a framework for doing mission and ministry in our time."[21]

The time that I spent between Christmas and New Year's Day on the Holy Island of Lindisfarne in 2002 praying, reading, hiking, and worshiping and in conversation with Ray Simpson (the founder and guardian of the new religious order of St. Aidan and Hilda, and the author of many informative books about Celtic Christianity) was formative. Earlier at Glendalough (the site of one of Ireland's best preserved and most notable early monastic cities) and also on the Holy Island, I discovered a whole new world of spiritual soul making. Clearly, the experience of the fourth through eleventh century Anglo-Saxon and Irish Church has much to teach us today. In the next section I will share what I learned.

Ruins of the Priory Church on Lindisfarne, the beginnings of which date back to St. Cuthbert in 773 A.D.
Photo by the author.

Guideposts of the Lindisfarne Pilgrim Way
Photo by the author.

Ruins of the Abbey Church at Whitby about 50 miles north of Lindisfarne.
Photo by the author.

Ed Leidel with Ray Simpson at Starbank Cottage on Lindisfarne.
Photo by Ira Leidel.

Exercises[22]

1. Reread Christian Schwartz's definition of a "healthy" and passionate spirituality. Where have you experienced that kind of spirituality in your personal life, or in a small group, or in your congregation? What was at the heart of that experience?

2. The day before St. Martin of Tours was confirmed he met a beggar who was freezing and without a coat. Filled with compassion, he cut his coat in two and gave half to the beggar. That night Martin had a dream where he experienced Jesus wrapped in the beggar's coat. Think of Martin as you reflect on the words of this Irish poem about hospitality.

> O King of the stars!
> Whether my house be dark or bright,
> Never shall it be closed to anyone,
> Lest Christ close his House against me.
>
> If there be a guest in your house
> And you conceal aught from him
> 'Tis not the guest that will be without it,
> But Jesus Mary's Son.
> (Meyer, 1928, p.100)

3. Reflect on these words by Dietrich Bonhoeffer from his book Life Together:

> Let him who cannot be alone beware of community...
> Let him who is not in community beware of being
> Alone...One who wants fellowship without solitude
> plunges into the void of words and feelings, and
> one seeks solitude without fellowship perishes
> in the abyss of vanity, self-infatuation and despair.
> (Bonhoeffer, 1952 pp. 77-8)

4. A good way to approach God is with someone in your heart: a good way to approach someone is with God in your heart. Listen to God on behalf of others: listen to others on behalf of God. Make sure you give your undivided attention to each one in their own right. Try to meet people and approach God this way for at least a week.

    (David Adam, 2003, pp.48-9)

Section Three
Searching for an Integrated Lifestyle: Breathing In and Breathing Out

---

There is an incredibly subtle and powerfully calculating industry of modern dislocation, where that which is deep and lives in the silence within us is completely ignored.... The inner world of the soul is suffering a great eviction by the landlord forces of advertising and external social reality.[23]

—John O'Donohue

St. John represents the way of contemplation; St. Peter the way of faithful action. They are "the male equivalents of Mary and Martha and as symbols between the contemplative and the active. This tension has always existed in the Church and we experience it ourselves in trying to find a balance between the inner and the outer. In this intensely materialistic and busy age, which sets great store by outward appearance and possessions and by activity, what is the balance that we need to recover in our spirituality, if we are to integrate the inner and the outer, and to allow the spiritual to shape our lives?"[24]

—Philip Newell

When Saint Patrick first entered Ireland as a teenage Saxon slave from 405-410 AD, he experienced a thoroughly pagan and agrarian world steeped in the bold and vivid stories of Celtic mythology and Druid wisdom which discerned meaning in life from the earth and from the stars. Though the son of an English priest, Patrick was not yet acquainted with the living power and presence of the One God manifest in a Trinity of Persons.

Called later by God in a dream, Patrick returns to the place of enslavement in 432 AD as one of the Christian Church's first missionary bishops to a pagan people. In the next 29 years of Patrick's missionary zeal, Ireland is amazingly transformed into a Christian nation without one drop of a martyr's blood being spilled. Thomas Cahill reveals a startling contrast in his popular How the Irish Saved Civilization:

> "Patrick's gift to the Irish was his Christianity—the first de-Romanized Christianity in human history, a Christianity without the sociological baggage of the Greco-Roman world, a Christianity that completely inculturated itself into the Irish scene…. Through the Edict of Milan, which had legalized the new religion in 313 and made it the new emperor's pet, Christianity had been received into Rome, not Rome into Christianity! Roman culture was little altered by the exchange, and it is arguable that Christianity lost much of its distinctiveness. But in the Patrician exchange, Ireland…had been received into Christianity, which transformed Ireland into something New, something never seen before—a Christian culture, where slavery and human sacrifice became unthinkable, and warfare, though impossible for humans to eradicate, diminished markedly."[25]

Whereas Rome transformed Christianity (for good and for ill), Christianity transformed Ireland. Unlike the Christianity of the Roman Empire, Irish Christianity formed around monastic communities of traveling monks. Ireland had no cities or even towns, but villages led by clan chieftains, and kings who ultimately divided Ireland into five geographic regions. In time it was the abbots and abbesses with their highly disciplined monks and nuns, not the bishops and priests, who became responsible for the Christianization of Ireland.

The monks and nuns, or *religieuse* as Peter Tremayne[26] calls them in his wonderful Sister Fidelma mystery series[27] of seventh-century Celtic Ireland, live the tension between a double commitment to both *place* and *pilgrimage*. Sister Fidelma, a member of the Celtic community of St. Bridget of Kildare, travels around Ireland, England and Italy with her soul-friend (*Anam Chara*), Brother Eadulf, a Saxon monk and envoy of the Archbishop of Canterbury. Together they bring their balanced gifts of Irish intuition and English practicality to expose complicated situations of murder, thievery, and political intrigue. In an idealistic way, Fidelma and Eadulf represent a working together of the classic Celtic/Roman, John/Peter, Mary/Martha, inner/outer, and even male/female tension, the lack of which has tended to divide the church into sectarian allegiances.

Irish monasticism is quite distinct from monasticism that develops in Western Europe. Its origins are in the Desert Fathers of Egypt and Syria. Celtic spirituality, which must always be seen in the context of Irish monasticism, bears much in common with Eastern Orthodox spirituality with its fascination with the desert and with iconic art and with human imagination. The qualities that give unique character to Celtic Christianity are:

(1) **Its holistic view of creation**. God is to be found in the "thin" places at the edges of civilization, where heaven and earth meet together. There is no separation between the sacred and the secular; between God and the world. The Celtic symbol of the circle suggests that reality has no beginning and no ending. Everything is connected. Its sense of integration with the animal world and with nature. Ireland is, after all, called the "Emerald Island"—a very green place.

Emerald Magic in Killarney Park

Round Tower at Glendalough

(2) **Its infatuation with the mystery of place**. Its holy wells, round towers and magnificent high crosses speak of God's incarnate and sacramental presence in unique and special places at the edges.

(3) **Its passion for pilgrimage**. God's Spirit leads wherever it will lead. To live in the Spirit is to be open to the Otherness that the pilgrimage discovers. St. Brendan the Navigator symbolizes this Celtic characteristic.

(4) **Its emphasis on belonging to a community of faith**. Without clan and family you had no identity. When you became a Christian you became a part of a monastic family, set apart from the greater society. God was truly experienced within the community.

(5) **Its attention to a therapeutic and healing pastoral care** through personal confession, penance, and fasting with a **soul-friend**. This caring characteristic also serves as its primary vehicle of evangelism. Continental monasticism (influenced by Augustine), in contrast, practiced public confession and stressed the importance of guilt and retribution.

(6) **Its intentional hospitality**. One wins the mind through the heart. Belief takes place in the context of community. Right relationship leads to right belief. Right belief leads finally to right behavior.

(7) **Its inclusion of the laity and women** in all roles. In contrast, continental Christianity held strongly to paternal, hierarchal structures.

(8) **Its playfulness with art and imagination** expressed in the creative iconography of the *Book of Kells* and the *Lindisfarne Gospels* with their ever-flowing interlaced lines, and its love for gab and story telling.

(9) **Its attention to everyday, mundane activity**, especially through prayer and blessing; George MacLeod calls this "**the Glory of the Grey.**" God is present in all things, not just on mountain tops and in the desert.

(10) **Its grassroots way of doing mission.** The Celtic heroes/heroines and their monastic followers sought out the people where they were, in contrast to the early Roman mission which tended to act as a chaplaincy to those who came to them. St. Aidan and others who followed him took time to be with individuals, drew out their concerns, and shared themselves, the gospel, and their worldly goods with them.[28]

Most all of these characteristics of a Christian life style are being sought today by a significant number of seekers, searching for a new way to live out their Christian faith. As many experience the traditional church losing its relevance, vitality, and numbers, the Celtic ideals provide a creative alternative for a more balanced and reformed Christianity.

Peter's Way overcomes John's Way

At the Council of Whitby in 664 a decisive victory was won over Celtic practices; giving precedence to Roman/Petrine customs. Specifically disputed were issues over the dating of Easter, the monastic tonsure or haircut, worship forms and spiritual disciplines over Celtic/Johanine customs. Some have interpreted this as a victory of a "law and order—faith and grace" over a "heart and mind—spirit and soul" expression of the Christian Way. Perhaps there is *some* truth to that interpretation of history. Certainly, there is a need today to balance the truth of both of these very valid spiritualities.

The Spiritual Life by Evelyn Underhill proposes that the spiritual life is an integration of (1) living in *communion* with God, and (2) living *co-operatively* with God.[29] It is both a breathing in (filling and receiving), and a breathing out (emptying and giving). Or, as the Psalmist (Psalm 121:8, BCP) says, "The Lord shall watch over your going out and your coming in, from this time forth for evermore."

It's both holding on and letting go; breathing in and breathing out; formation and mission; valuing order, while valuing the creative potential of chaos. With our roots in the past, we leaf out to the future. We are formed in Christ, and we give our lives away as Christ's Body. It's a bit like dancing, a two step dance. This attitudinal faith stance which generates a healthy spiritual life is more of an art than a skill. It really is like dancing. And there are two essential movements or steps to the dance. The right foot step is "holding on." The left foot step is "letting go." The art of leading from a faithful attitude has to do with getting the rhythm right between holding on and letting go.

David Adam, who retired as the Vicar of Lindisfarne while I was writing this Guide, has written a gem of a book about five Celtic Christian saints. All of these exemplars of Christianity danced the "two-step dance."

> Ninian's cave at Glasserton and *Candida Casa* ["White House," the monastery's worship hall] point to a rhythm of life that moved between activity and outreach and then a return to stillness and solitude: a balance between serving people and worshiping God. It is popular to say that the Church exists for mission; this is only a half truth for the Church exists to worship God and to give glory to him. The hyperactive Church is in danger of offering itself and a way of being busy without reference to God: even some study groups are in danger of talking more about God than they ever talk to him.[30]

William Countryman sees something very Anglican in a spirituality that maintains this dialectic between emptiness and fullness:

> "The dialectic of absence and presence lies at the heart of the poetic tradition of Anglican spirituality.... We might think of it as 'soul' of this spirituality, the life force that gives energy and movement to the rest.... But the enjoyment of presence is not the constant state of humanity here and now. It comes upon us, does its work, we return to some less exalted state or even to the experience of absence. But we are transformed.[31]

God's Grace keeps the creative tension going. We are surprised by Grace, accept it and journey on to be surprised yet again.

Exercises:

1.   Mentally divide your average day into three, eight hour sections. Assuming you sleep for about eight of those 24 hours, how much of the remaining sixteen hours is spent in quiet solitude where you are alone and not responding to any outside stimulus, and how much of your waking time is spent in active work, conversation, or physical exercise where you are responding in some way to your external environment? Draw a line down the middle of a page and list all of your quiet, introspective and introverted "activities" on the left, and your extraverted, interpersonal activities on the right. Give hourly time periods to each activity you list. How do the two sides balance out? How do they integrate with one another? Does each side feed the other? If you discover an overwhelming imbalance, ponder what effect that may be having on your overall health, and especially on your spiritual well-being.

2.   Calculate how much time you spent yesterday on each of the following:
     a. Work at home.
     b. Work out of the home.
     c. Time with your family, not including meal time.
     d. Social time with friends.
     e. Eating.
     f. Reading or studying.
     g. Praying (personal or corporate).
     h. Sleeping.
     i. Watching television, or listening to the radio, or to music.
     j. Exercising or walking.
     k. Time running errands.
     l. Just being still, with no task to be done, or expectations on your time—This could be time where you place your self in God's presence, or just a time of being still and relaxing.

Where did you spend *most* of your time, and the *least* of your time? Each personality type and vocation will require different distributions of time. The point here is whether or not you feel fulfilled in your life, and whether you experience "joy and wonder" in your work and play. Considering the discussion in this section, how would you judge your overall stewardship of time? Share the outcome of this exercise with a friend.

3.   Meditate (or journal) on these words:

Apprehend God in all things, for God is in all things, the single creature is full of God and is a book about God. Every creature is a word of God. If I spent enough time with even the tiniest of creatures—even a caterpillar—I would never have to prepare a sermon. So full of God is every creature.

(Meister Eckhart)

Section Four

Four Gateways
to the Presence of Soul

Each of us needs to learn the unique language of our soul. In the distinctive language, we will discover a lens of thought to brighten and illuminate our inner world.[32]

—John O'Donohue

So far we have suggested that to be re-awakened to a Celtic, passionate spirituality, there must first come a hunger and thirst for it; a desire for conversion, born in repentance and tears. We have also suggested that there is a need to return today to a more balanced life in the spirit, where, like the Celtic Christians of a bygone age, we bring back more prominently the elements of silence, asceticism, place and pilgrimage, and imagination to counterbalance our over active lives.

But how does one enter this unfamiliar territory of the spirit? After tears, where does one go? Where are the gates to the inner life of the soul?

In trying to explain the spiritual life, both Alan Jones and John Westerhoff[33] make interesting use of Graham Greene's novel <u>Dr. Fisher of Geneva, or the Bomb Party</u>.

> "Greene describes the four requirements necessary for human beings to live in an ever deepening and loving relationship to God....
>
> Greene's hero is talking with his wife about her malicious father, Dr. Fisher, and his strange friends. She asks, 'Have you a soul?'
>
> I think I have one—shop worn but still there, but if souls exist you certainly have one.'
>
> 'Why?'
>
> 'You've suffered.'
>
> One of Dr. Fisher's friends is Monsieur Belmont, a busy lawyer who specializes in tax evasion. As for a soul, 'he hasn't time to develop one.... A soul requires a private life. Belmont has no time for a private life.
>
> There is also a soldier, the Divisionaire, who 'might possibly have a soul. There's something unhappy about him.'
>
> 'And Mr. Kips?'
>
> 'I'm not sure about him either. There's a sense of disappointment about him. He might be looking for something he mislaid. Perhaps he's looking for his soul and not a dollar.'
>
> Then there is Richard Deane, the aging movie idol. 'No, definitely not. No soul. I'm told he has copies of his old films and he plays them over every night to himself.... He's satisfied with himself. If you have a soul you can't be satisfied.'
>
> Last there is Dr. Fisher himself, who unlike his hideous friends appears possibly to have satisfied these three requirements.
>
> 'And my father?' she asks.
>
> He has a soul all right, but I think it's a damned one.'
>
> There we have Graham Greene's four requirements for living a spiritual life: a willingness to embrace suffering [Dr. Greene's hero], our own and the world's; a life marked by moments of silence and solitude [unlike Belmont]; a willingness to pay attention to the deep restlessness

in our spirits [Mr. Kips]; and life within a community of faith [Dr. Fisher] that sees the image of God, the image of Christ, in us."

Each of Greene's characters has a uniquely different window into their soul. Dr. Greene's hero embraces suffering (sensate awareness); Monsieur Belmont rejects the private world of introspection (thinking processing); Mr. Kips appears to have the gift of a deeply restless spirit (intuitive awareness); and lastly, Dr. Fisher values his community of friends (feeling processing).

Interestingly, these four gateways to having a soul life, mirror the four dominant functions of (1) intuition, (2) sensing, (3) thinking and (4) feeling, discerned by Carl Jung in the early twentieth century, and brought to practical application to us today through the Myer-Briggs Type Indicator—a personality inventory which purports to show the constellation of a person's innate giftedness, described in one of sixteen personality types. For more detail, see Appendix B at the end of this guide which provides a summary of Jung's Type Dynamic Theory.

Each of us is created uniquely in the image of God. Jung discovered that this genetic uniqueness can be categorized to show how (while remaining totally unique) each of us can be placed along side others who have similar behavior tendencies, and therefore similar tendencies to live out different spiritual behaviors.

A number of writers about the spiritual life[34] have used these Jungian function categories to describe four historical schools of spirituality, as well as describing different ways that different personality types use to discover God and live a spiritual life. Various instruments can be administered[35] to discern which of the four types coincides with your own gateway to your soul life with God.

The idea behind this way of looking at the terrain of your soul is that your dominant function (body-sensing, or spirit-intuition, or head-thinking, or heart-feeling) is the way you consciously lead in your perceiving (sensing and intuiting), and the way you make decisions (thinking and feeling). This psychology of behavior is mirrored in scripture as Jesus quotes the Old Testament in exhorting us to:

> "Love the Lord your God with all your heart [feeling], and with all your soul [intuition], and with all your mind [thinking], and with all your strength [sensing]." Mark 12:30

Everyone uses all of these aspects of our personality, but it is the dominant function that takes the first step in driving our conscious behavior. Contrariwise, each dominant function has a corresponding inferior (Jung's word) function which dominates our unconscious and dream world. It is through our inferior function (*also* either sensing, intuiting, thinking or feeling) that we tend to experience God in amazing and usually surprising experiences of Grace. For a brief introduction and summary of Jung's type dynamic theory see Appendix A at the end of this

Guide. For the purposes of this Guide, the following descriptions will be used for the four soul types: (1) *sacramental* for personalities are gifted with sensual perception; (2) *mystical* for those personalities that are gifted with intuitive perception; (3) *prophetic* for those personalities that are gifted with thinking decision making; and (4) *communal* for those personalities that are gifted with feeling decision making.

In Ferbane, County Ottaly, Ireland there is a high cross called the Gallen Priory Cross which is thought to date back to 950 A.D.

The Celtic Cross is known throughout the world as the emblem of Celtic Christianity and it can be considered the symbol of Celtic-ness itself. Celtic Crosses began to appear during the fifth century A.D., its shape is derived from a pagan sun symbol, the sun wheel, which later became a symbol of the Christian Godhead. The sun wheel was originally a cross surrounded by a circle with a center stone representing the sun and mock suns at the four quarters. The stone at the center of the circle also represents the navel of the world. The cross represents eternal life; its horizontal axis being the earthly world and the vertical axis the heavenly world coming together as the union of Heaven and Earth. Celtic Crosses are imbued with continuous and interwoven knot and spiral motifs symbolizing the continuity of life, death and rebirth. Celtic Crosses often have images of the Christian crucifixion, patriarchs and saints.

The Gallen Cross, an unusual cross of the Christian period, can be viewed in the grounds of Gallen Priory, together with a collection of early Christian grave slabs. The Priory, once a landlord's residence and later a novitiate of the St. Joseph of Cluny Order, is now a nursing home.

The Wild Goose Studio sells reproductions of the Gallen Priory cross. On the back of the cross is an interpretation of the four heads of the cross, which are said to represent Adam (thinking-bottom), Eve (feeling-top), Cain (intuition-right side/left hand-right brain), and Abel (sensation-left side/right brain).

Each of these "personality types" is a gate way to the central God-Head Spiral. The heads are connected to the center by serpent heads possibly representing dreams or prayer channels to the God-Head. The Gallen cross gives us a metaphor of the arms of the arms, head and torso of Christ drawing us into the Godhead symbolized in the cross's central and outer circles.

The chart on the next page integrates the wild Goose studios intuitive interpretation of the cross with contemporary names given to four schools of spirituality.

Soul Types: Gateways to God

Gallen Priory Cross (11th c.)	Carl Jung (1938)	Urban Holmes (1980)	John Westerhoff (1994)	Corinne Ware (1995)	John Ackermann (2001)	Ed Leidel (2003)
Cain	Sensing	Speculative-Kataphatic	Sacramental	Head Spirituality	Thinking	Sacramental Soul Type
Eve	Feeling	Affective-Kataphatic	Charismatic	Heart Spirituality	Feeling	Communal Soul Type
Abel	Intuitive	Affective-Apophatic	Mystical	Mystical Spirituality	Being	Mystical Soul Type
Adam	Thinking	Speculative-Apophatic	Apostolic	Visionary Spirituality	Doing	Prophetic Soul Type

Gallen Priory Cross
The Wild Goose Studio

Humankind, while standing on reason, wrestles with unconscious energy.

♦ At centre a sun spiral = for the Celts the sun was the life source.
  Uncoiling serpents = the unconscious: dreams, myths, archetypes, etc.

♦ Four heads = Adam & Eve, Cain & Abel; or **Thinking & Feeling, Sensation & Intuition.**

♦ Linear pattern at base = reason, oscience, logos.

♦ Spiral circle joining the heads = unity, harmony, and love.

Cast by hand at Kinsale, co.coxh, Ireland # 32
From 10c. carving, co. offaly

The following exercise will help you to discern which of these spiritualities best fits your soul type.

Corinne Ware's Spiritual Type Sorter[36]

Circle the most descriptive sentence in each of the following categories. Add up the sum of each of the numbers and place the four scores in the boxes at the end of this exercise.

The Order of Worship
1. A carefully planned and orderly worship program is a glory to God.
2. A deeply moving and spontaneous meeting is a glory to God.
3. Simplicity and some silence are important elements needed for worship.
4. It is not a service, but ordering ourselves to God's service that is important.

Time
1. Stick to announced beginning and ending times of worship services.
2. It is important to extend the meeting time if one feels led to do so.
3. All time is God's time. A sense of timelessness is important.
4. Gather whenever and for as long as you need to accomplish the task.

Prayer
1. Words express poetic praise; we ask for knowledge and guidance.
2. Let words and feelings evoke God's presence in this moment.
3. Empty the mind of distractions and simply be in the presence of the holy.
4. My life and my work are my prayer.

Music
1. Music and text express praise to God and belief about God.
2. Singing warms and unites us and expresses the soul's deepest heart.
3. Chant and tone bring the soul to quietness and union with God.
4. Songs can mobilize and inspire to greater effort and dedication.

Preaching
1. The word of God, rightly proclaimed, is the centerpiece of worship.
2. The gospel, movingly preached, is the power of God to change lives.
3. Proclamation is heard when the Spirit of God speaks to the inward heart.
4. What we do is our "preaching" and speaks louder than anything we say.

Emphasis
1. A central purpose is that we fulfill our vocation (calling) in the world.
2. A central purpose is that we learn to walk in holiness with the Lord.
3. A central purpose is that we be one with the creator.
4. A central purpose is that we obey God's will completely.

Support of Causes
(If necessary, circle the words that apply and note categories with the most circles.)
1. Support seminaries, publishing houses, scholarship, preaching to others.
2. Support evangelism, missions, spreading the word on television and radio.
3. Support places of retreat, spiritual direction, and liturgical reform.
4. Support political action to establish justice in society and its institutions.

Criticism
1. Sometimes I/we are said to be too intellectual, dogmatic, and "dry."
2. Sometimes I/we are said to be too emotional, dogmatic, and anti-intellectual.
3. Sometimes I/we are said to be escaping from the world and are not being realistic.
4. Sometimes I/we are said to have tunnel vision and to be too moralistic.

Dominating Themes
(If necessary, circle the words that apply and note categories with the most circles.)
1. Discernment, discipline, knowledge, order, grace, justification.
2. Love, conversion, witness, spontaneity, sanctification.
3. Poverty, humility, wisdom, letting go, transcendence.
4. Simplicity, purity of heart, action, temperance, obedience, martyrdom.

Member Criteria
What the congregation believes is necessary, what you believe is necessary.
1. Assent to doctrine; baptism; endorsement by group.
2. A personal inward experience of God, baptism; public declaration.
3. All who face Godward are incorporated in the holy.
4. Solidarity with humankind is membership in God's kingdom.

Ritual and Liturgy
1. Ritual and liturgy evoke memory and presence, teaching traditional truths.
2. Liturgy and ritual ceremonies are not of great importance.
3. Ritual and liturgy are ways in which God becomes present to us.
4. Ritual and liturgy are one way we make statements about inner conviction.

Concept of God
1. God is revealed in Scripture, sacrament, and in Jesus Christ and his cross.
2. I can feel that God is real and that Christ lives in my heart.
3. God is mystery and can be grasped for, but not completely known.
4. We participate in the mystery of God when we become creators with God in the world.

Sum of # 1's	Sum of # 2's	Sum of #3's	Sum of # 4's

1: **Sacramental Soul Type** (Myers Briggs S types: ISTJ, ISFJ, ESTP & ESFP)
2: **Communal Soul Type** (Myers Briggs F types: ISFP, INFP, ESFJ & ENFJ)
3: **Mystical Soul Type** (Myers Briggs N types: INFJ, INTJ, ENFP & ENTP)
4. **Prophetic Soul Type** (Myers Briggs T types: ISTP, INTP, ESTJ & ENTJ)

My Preferred Soul Type is _____

My Secondary Soul Type is _____

Soul Type 1: Sacramental Spirituality

This is a spirituality of the body. Those individuals whose dominant function is sensing, and whose inferior function is intuition, belong to the spirituality type that is sacramental. In Graham Greene's novel this soul type is characterized by the capacity to mature through suffering. Life and God are experienced especially in a physical, bodily form. Prayer is sensuous and direct. Incense, color, statutes, and processions are helpful expressions of worship. Liturgically, the sacramental soul type experiences the sacramental (concrete) character of the Eucharist and prefers instructional sermons. Attention to detail, order and control are important. Obedience and faith are primary virtues. Fulfillment is especially experienced by serving others. God is experienced as a Rock, as one who is present in order, ritual, and beauty. God is revealed through institutions, doctrines and concrete data. The preferred Gospel of this soul type is Matthew. The approach to the bible tends to be practical and literal. The sacramental soul journeyer seeks faithfulness, obedience and physical harmony.

John Westerhoff characterizes this school of spirituality as:

> ...dominated by mental prayer or meditation, a process of engaging the senses in reflecting on or musing over an experience of a painting, a poem, a piece of music, or the scriptures. The rosary is a mental prayer that combines familiar, repetitive prayers with meditations on the joyful, sorrowful, and glorious mysteries of the Christian faith (the incarnation, crucifixion, resurrection and ascension), which are all to communicate depths of spiritual meaning beyond the obvious.
>
> Meditative prayers for dealing with disordered affections are another example of this kind of prayer. In prayers for disordered affections, if, for example, we are angry, we take the person we are angry with before God and in our imagination speak and act out our anger until we can do so no longer. Then we are silent so that God can fill the open space we have created in our minds with God's love. [37]

In ministry environments, sacramentalists:
- are aware of the uniqueness of each event
- focus on what works
- like an established way of doing things
- enjoy applying what they have already learned
- work steadily with a realistic idea of how long things will take

- reach a conclusion step by step
- are careful about the facts
- accept current reality as a given to work with.

In desert experiences, sacramentalists:
- often feel incompetent and have confused vision
- are overwhelmed with feelings of ambiguity
- tend towards controlling and complaining behavior and excessive conformity when stressed
- experience Grace intuitively

Roman Catholicism especially typifies this way of soul life, though it is present in all denominations. St. Peter is its patron saint. Other historic exemplars of this spirituality are Ignatius of Loyola, Martin Luther, Augustine and Dag Hammarskjold.

ATTRIBUTE	The SACRAMENTAL SOUL
	SENSING (S)
Soul's preferred Language	The Body
Patron Saint	Peter
Historic personages	Ignatius of Loyola, Martin Luther, Augustine, Dag Hammarskjold
Christian Ethos	Roman Catholic and Doctrinal Churches
Prayer	Sensuous
Preference for	Sensory reality, details, status quo
Virtue	Faith
	Obedience
Significant aspects of Reality	Immediacy, concreteness
Natural Spiritual Path	Service
Windows of Revelation	Society, institutions, data
Aspects of God	Incarnation, Rock, Order, Beauty, Grace, Ritual, Sacrament
Roles of God	Emmanuel, Crucified One, Incarnate, Presence
Approach to Bible	Practical, literal
Favorite Gospel	Matthew
Liturgical preference	Eucharist as sacrifice, instructional sermons, processions, incense, color, statues,
Seeks (heaven)	Faithfulness, obedience physical harmony
Gateway	Suffering, passion, tears
Deserts	Confused Vision & Incompetence
Dream/Grace Language (inferior function)	Intuition (N) = *the shadow of S*
Vice Tendencies	Pride & Sloth
Pitfalls & Negative Tendencies	Idolatry, excessive conformity, controlling, complaining
Achilles' Heal	Ambiguity
Needs for Growth	Awareness

Soul Type 2: Communal Spirituality

This is a spirituality of the heart. Those individuals whose dominant function is feeling, and whose inferior function is thinking, belong to the spirituality type that is communal. This type is a mirror image of the prophetic soul type. In Graham Green's novel this soul type is Dr. Fisher himself, as he seeks to live his life of faith in the community of his friends. Life and God are experienced especially in groups through relationships and through feeling. Prayer is of the heart as it seeks God's presence, unity, connectedness, and mercy. Liturgically, the communal soul type experiences the Eucharist as a "holy communion," enjoys inspirational sermons, the passing of the Peace and is especially sensitive to the absolution of sins. Love and chastity are its most highly valued virtues. Fulfillment is achieved through the realization of ideals. God is experienced as Lover, Redeemer, Savior and as Abba. God is consciously revealed through cherished relationships. The preferred gospel of this soul type is Luke. The approach to the bible is personal and immediate. Communal types seek communion, appreciation and personal harmony.

Westerhoff calls this the charismatic type and he characterizes this school of spirituality as:

> This school is dominated by verbal-sensate prayer. Here the whole body, all of the senses-speaking, tasting, touching, smelling, and listening-and the emotions, is involved. It can take the form of beautiful vocal prayers, whether they are contained in prayer books, written originally, or spoken spontaneously. This type of praying begins with adoration (I love you, God) and continues with praise (you are ever-forgiving), thanksgiving (I am grateful for…), oblation (I give my life to you), contrition (I am sorry for…), intercession (please do…for…), and last, petition (I desire…). It can take the form of chanting the Psalms or singing gospel hymns.
>
> Another example from this school is the devotion known as the Way of the Cross. In this devotion persons, alone or with others, walk the trying, painful Via Dolorosa with Jesus, singing and stopping along the way at fourteen stations to listen to the scriptures and pray, so as to experience and emotionally identify with Jesus' actions on our behalf in order that we might learn to follow in the way of the cross.
>
> Prayer that involves clapping, touching, body movement, shouting, and the free expression of emotion is typical of the affective-kataphatic school. Different racial and ethnic groups have different cultural manifestations of these devotional activities and may appear radically different.

For example, an African-American gospel hymn sung with spontaneous prayers and an Anglo-Catholic evensong with ancient written prayers both emerge from the same school of spirituality.[38]

In ministry environments, communal types:
- like harmony and will work to make it happen
- are good at seeing the effects of choices on people
- tend to be sympathetic
- enjoy pleasing people
- take an interest in the person behind the job or idea
- respond to other's values

In desert experiences, communal souls:
- experience meaninglessness and trustless-ness in the midst of conflict and estrangement
- tend to romanticizing, blaming and grudge bearing
- may experience anger and jealousy

The primary aim of communal soul types is to achieve holiness of life and friendship with Jesus. They yearn for experiences of the outpouring of God's spirit in the midst of their communal life. Historic personages of spirituality are Benedict of Nursia, Julian of Norwich, John Wesley, George Herbert, and Martin Luther King, Jr.

	The COMMUNAL (Charismatic) Soul
Attribute	**FEELING**
Soul's preferred Language	The Heart
Patron Saint	Mary
Historic personages	Benedict of Nursia, Julian of Norwich, John Wesley, George Herbert, Martin Luther King, Jr.
Christian Ethos	Methodist, Baptist, Evangelical Churches
Prayer	Affective
Preference for	Subjective values
Virtue	Love
	Chastity
Significant aspects of Reality	Feelings, memory, the ideal
Natural Spiritual Path	Devotion
Windows of Revelation	Relationships, emotions, groups
Aspects of God	Relational, Familial, Presence, Unity, Connection, Mercy
Roles of God	Lover, Redeemer, Savior, Abba
Approach to Bible	Personal, immediate
Favorite Gospel	Luke
Liturgical preference	Eucharist as communion, inspirational sermons, the Peace, absolution
Seeks (heaven)	Communion, appreciation, personal harmony
Gateway	Disconnected-ness
Deserts	Meaninglessness & Trustlessness
Dream/Grace Language (inferior function)	Thinking (T) = *the shadow of F*
Vice Tendencies	Jealousy & Anger
Pitfalls & Negative Tendencies	Romanticizing, blaming, grudge bearing
Achilles' Heal	Conflict, estrangement
Needs for Growth	Knowledge

Soul Type 3: Mystical Spirituality

This is a spirituality of the spirit. Those individuals whose dominant function is intuition, and whose inferior function is sensing, belong to a spirituality type that is mystical. This type is the mirror image of the sacramentalist type. In Graham Green's novel this soul type is characterized by a life that marked by moments of silence and solitude. Life and God are experienced especially through the imagination. Prayer is intuitive, seeking a vision that is cosmic and oceanic. Icons, silence, incense and music are helpful to this type's worship experience. Liturgically, the mystical soul journeyer experiences the Eucharist as mystical drama, and prefers metaphorical (story telling) sermons. Mystics seek possibilities, patterns, and creative transformation. Hope and poverty (detachment) are valued virtues. Fulfillment is especially realized in new awareness—in "aha" experiences. God is experienced as mystery, light, glory, creator, and connecter. God is revealed through dream, metaphor, and insight. The preferred gospel of this soul type is John. The approach to the bible is symbolic and metaphorical. The mystic seeks union with God, integration with nature, and aesthetic harmony.

Westerhoff characterizes this school of spirituality as:

> ...dominated by contemplative prayer. Centering prayers are typical. Their purpose is to occupy and free the mind so that one may dwell with God. The rattling off of prayers known by heart can achieve the same purpose. The oldest prayers in the church are centering prayers such as "Lord Jesus, Son of God, have mercy on me, a sinner." Listening to Eastern music that has no set rhythm or story line; fantasy exercises; gazing on an icon…. Often people are confused about this school because it includes both the Quakers and the eastern Orthodox. What we need to remember is that both have the same end, the emptying of the self from all distractions so as to be fully aware of the Holy Spirit and its activity in our lives. [Quakers] do this by creating empty, white space where there is nothing to stimulate the senses and silence rules. [The Eastern Orthodox] make use of the senses as a means of eliminating their influence. For example, Western painting, music and incense are intended to stimulate our senses, but within the Eastern Orthodox Church, the icon, music and incense are intended to do the opposite. One gazes on an icon to be taken through it, so as to make direct contact with the mystery that is spiritually present but hidden.[39]

In ministry environments, mystics:
- are aware of new challenges and possibilities
- focus on how things could be improved
- dislike doing the same thing repeatedly
- enjoy learning new skills
- work in bursts of new energy powered by enthusiasm
- follow their inspirations and hunches
- ask why things are as they are

In desert experiences, mystics:
- feel confused by details
- feel that they are in a boundary-less environment
- are overwhelmed by restrictions and repetition
- become impractical, and misread small details when stressed
- experience Grace sensually

The ancient Celtic Church, Anglicanism and Eastern Orthodoxy typify this way of soul life. St. John the Apostle and Evangelist is its patron saint. Other historic exemplars of this spirituality are Teresa of Avila, John of the Cross, Thomas Merton, St. Aidan, St. Cuthbert, and St. Bridget.

	The MYSTICAL Soul
Attribute	INTUITION
Soul's preferred Language	The Spirit
Patron Saint	John
Historic personages	Teresa of Avila, John of the Cross, Thomas Munzer, Thomas Merton, Howard Thurman, George Fox, & most of E. Orthodox & Celtic spirituality
Christian Ethos	Eastern Orthodox and Anglican (Celtic) Churches
Prayer	Symbolic
Preference for	Possibilities, patterns and change
Virtue	Hope
	Poverty
Significant aspects of Reality	Anticipation, vision
Natural Spiritual Path	Awareness
Windows of Revelation	Insight, imagination, dreams
Aspects of God	Mystery, Holy Spirit, Inspiration, Glory, Light, Desert, Creation, Nature
Roles of God	Creator, Logos, Vision Caster, Story Teller
Approach to Bible	Symbolic, metaphorical
Favorite Gospel	John
Liturgical preference	Eucharistic as mystery, metaphorical sermons, stories, Sanctus, Gloria, incense, icons
Seeks (heaven)	Mystical union, integration aesthetic harmony
Gateway	Silence
Deserts	Non-Sense & Boundary-lessness
Dream/Grace Language (inferior function)	Sensing (S) = *the shadow of N*
Vice Tendencies	Gluttony & Lust
Pitfalls & Negative Tendencies	Impracticality, illusion, awareness of details
Achilles' Heal	Restriction, repetition
Needs for Growth	Service

Soul Type 4: Prophetic Spirituality

This is a spirituality of the mind. Those individuals whose dominant function is thinking, and whose inferior function is feeling, belong to the spirituality type that is prophetic. In Graham Green's novel this soul type is characterized by the restless searching of Dr. Kips for intellectual truth. Life and God are experienced especially through processes of critical thinking. Prayer is mental, cognitive, many layered and often complex. Liturgically, the prophetic soul journeyer experiences the Eucharist as a gathering of all of God's creatures (rich and poor, "ins" and "outs," young and old, etc.) where justice and forgiveness come together. Good liturgy contains theologically sound sermons, intercessions for justice and a prophetic dismissal to go out into the world to do healing and restoration. Prophetic types seek first principles, justice, restitution, and reconciliation. Justice and truth are valued virtues. Fulfillment is especially realized in the reasoned apprehension of new knowledge. God is experienced as First Cause, the Word, Judge, Messiah, Prophet and All Goodness. God is revealed through reason, speculation, and logic. The preferred Gospel of this soul type is Mark. The approach to the bible is analytical and abstract. The prophetic type seeks enlightenment, justice, truth, and conceptual harmony.

Westerhoff characterizes this school of spirituality as:

> ...dominated by active prayer. [He calls this the apostolic type. I prefer to call it prophetic, as followers of this way of spirituality have an inclination to envision change.] This school is dominated by active prayer. For many, this is the most difficult to understand. Spiritual reading, listening to quiet day homilies, taking a hike, playing music, drawing, and dancing in silence are forms of active prayer. So are fasting, the giving of alms, and the performance of acts of mercy. While for most people such acts are a response to devotional prayer, for those in this school, they are the prayer itself. For example, one might have a friend who is having a problem with alcohol. A responsible prayer for someone in this school of spirituality would be for the person who is praying to stop drinking alcoholic beverages but not to tell the alcoholic friend of his or her concern, because that would be manipulation and not prayer. The prayer is one's own action on a friend's behalf.

> One devotion from this school concerns a way to pray the Lord's Prayer based on the understanding that each phrase is intended to be a question that we are to bring to God each day. Thus we can be aware of how God would like us to behave and, having responded appropriately,

receive the power to do so. The following questions, for example, are derived from the Lord's Prayer and prompt emulation: "What do you want to make holy and whole in my life this day?" "How can your reign come through me this day?" "For what do I need to be forgiven, and with whom do I need to be reconciled?"[40]

In ministry environments, Prophet types:
- are good at putting things in logical order
- able to anticipate logical outcomes of choices
- tend to be firm and tough minded
- are able to reprimand people when necessary
- have a talent for analyzing a problem
- need to be treated fairly

In desert experiences, prophet types:
- may experience powerlessness and loneliness
- may tend to cynicism, dogmatism, and impatience
- are overwhelmed by inconsistencies and ignorance
- Grace is experienced through feeling.

The primary aim of the prophetic type is to obey God's Will completely. Its major concern is to witness to God's reign. It is a spirituality that teaches spirituality and includes such historic persons as Dominic, John Calvin, Catherine of Genoa, and Dorothy Day.

The following charts describe the character and interaction of the dominant and inferior functions in more detail:

	The PROPHETIC (Apostolic) Soul
Attribute	**THINKING**
Soul's preferred Language	The Mind
Patron Saint	Paul
Historic personages	Dominic, John Calvin, Catherine of Genoa, Dorothy Day
Christian Ethos	Reformed and Confessional Churches
Prayer	Cognitive
Preference for	Objective values
Virtue	Justice
	Truth
Significant aspects of Reality	Theory, principles
Natural Spiritual Path	Knowledge
Windows of Revelation	Reason, speculation, logic
Aspects of God	First Cause, Principle, Word, Goodness, Special Revelation
Roles of God	Judge, Messiah, Truth, Prophet
Approach to Bible	Analytical, abstract
Favorite Gospel	Mark
Liturgical preference	Theological sermons, the dismissal into the world, intercessions for justice
Seeks (heaven)	Enlightenment, justice, truth, conceptual harmony
Gateway	Unrest
Deserts	Powerlessness & Loneliness
Dream/Grace Language (inferior function)	Feeling (F) = *the shadow of T*
Vice Tendencies	Bitterness & Covetousness
Pitfalls & Negative Tendencies	Cynicism, dogmatism, impatience
Achilles' Heal	Inconsistency & ignorance
Needs for Growth	Devotion

Summary Chart

ATTRIBUTE	SENSING (S)	INTUITION (N)	THINKING (T)	FEELING (F)
Soul's preferred Language/Functionality	The Body	The Spirit	The Mind	The Heart
School of Spirituality	Sacramental	Mystical	Prophetic/Apostolic	Communal/Charismatic
Patron Saint	Peter	John	Paul	Mary
Historic personages	Ignatius of Loyola, Martin Luther, Augustine, Dag Hammarskjold	Teresa of Avila, John of the Cross, Thomas Munzer, Thomas Merton, Howard Thurman, George Fox, & most of E. Orthodox & Celtic spirituality	Dominic, John Calvin, Catherine of Genoa, Dorothy Day	Benedict of Nursia, Julian of Norwich, John Wesley, George Herbert, Martin Luther King, Jr.
Christian Ethos	Roman Catholic and Doctrinal Churches	Eastern Orthodox and Anglican (Celtic) Churches	Reformed and Confessional Churches	Methodist, Baptist, Evangelical Churches
Prayer	Sensuous	Symbolic	Cognitive	Affective
Preference for	Sensory reality, details, status quo	Possibilities, patterns, and change	Objective values	Subjective values
Virtue	Faith	Hope	Justice	Love
	Obedience	Poverty	Truth	Chastity
Significant aspects of Reality	Immediacy, concreteness	Anticipation, vision	Theory, principles	Feelings, memory, the ideal
Natural Spiritual Path	Service	Awareness	Knowledge	Devotion
Windows of Revelation	Society, institutions, data	Insight, imagination, dreams	Reason, speculation, logic	Relationships, emotions, groups
Aspects of God	Incarnation, Rock, Order, Beauty, Grace, Ritual, Sacrament	Mystery, Holy Spirit, Inspiration, Glory, Light, Desert, Creation, Nature	First Cause, Principle, Word, Goodness, Special Revelation	Relational, Familial, Presence, Unity, Connection, Mercy
Roles of God	Emmanuel, Crucified One, Incarnate, Presence	Creator, Logos, Vision Caster, Story Teller	Judge, Messiah, Truth, Prophet	Lover, Redeemer, Savior, Abba
Approach to Bible	Practical, literal	Symbolic, metaphorical	Analytical, abstract	Personal, immediate
Favorite Gospel	Matthew	John	Mark	Luke
Liturgical preference	Eucharist as sacrifice, instructional sermons, processions, incense, color, statues	Eucharistic as mystery, metaphorical sermons, stories, Sanctus, Gloria, incense, icons	Theological sermons, the dismissal into the world, intercessions for justice	Eucharist as communion, inspirational sermons, the Peace, absolution
Seeks (heaven)	Faithfulness, obedience, physical harmony	Mystical union, integration, aesthetic harmony	Enlightenment, justice, truth, conceptual harmony	Communion, appreciation, personal harmony
Gateway	Suffering, passion, tears	Silence	Unrest	Disconnected-ness
Deserts	Confused Vision & Incompetence	Non-Sense & Boundary-lessness	Powerlessness & Loneliness	Meaninglessness & Trustlessness
Dream/Grace Language (inferior function)	Intuition (N) = *the shadow of S*	Sensing (S) = *the shadow of N*	Feeling (F) = *the shadow of T*	Thinking (T) = *the shadow of F*
Vice Tendencies	Pride & Sloth	Gluttony & Lust	Bitterness & Covetousness	Jealousy & Anger
Pitfalls & Negative Tendencies	Idolatry, excessive conformity, controlling, complaining	Impracticality, illusion, awareness of details	Cynicism, dogmatism, impatience	Romanticizing, blaming, grudge bearing
Achilles' Heal	Ambiguity	Restriction, repetition	Inconsistency & ignorance	Conflict, estrangement
Needs for Growth	Awareness	Service	Devotion	Knowledge

If you ever have the opportunity to participate in a retreat with others where you work at discerning your unique spiritual terrain, you will be richly rewarded by gathering in groups with others who have your same spiritual tendencies. You will be inevitably encouraged by the discovery of how alike your desert and mountain top experiences are. Sharing experiences in such a group will often bring new learnings about how to deepen your spiritual life and how to grow from your experiences of adversary.

Similarly, an awareness of one's own spiritual terrain and of the possibilities that exist for others helps one to become more accepting and appreciative of those whose spiritual approach is by another route.

Exercises:

1. Determine which of the four prayer languages (soul-types) fits your personality. Can you think of a friend who shares some of the same personality and spiritual tendencies that you have? If such a person comes to mind, consider sharing the information in this section with him or her, and learn from one another about your different "desert experiences" as well as your different "wells of grace" experiences.

2. Purchase or check out from the library some of the spiritual "classics" authored by one or two of the historic personages mentioned in the *Soul's Qualities & Tendencies* chart that seem attractive or compatible with your spiritual temperament.

Section Five

Eight Deserts and Wells of Grace: Towards Developing a Phenomenology for Soul Life

*Maybe it is time now for a phenomenology of soul. The soul creates, shapes, and peoples our inner life. The gateway to our deepest identity is not through mechanical analysis. We need to listen to the soul and articulate its wisdom in a poetic and mystical form. To awaken the soul is to travel to the frontier where experience bows down before the **mysterium tremendum et fascinans** of Otherness.[41]*
—John O'Donohue

Life is like a whirlwind. That's what most of feel about our lives these days. Things are changing so fast. It no longer seems possible to be fully in control of our affairs. Contemporary scientists tell us that the universe is really not the orderly, predictable place that we once thought it was. There is chaos and uncertainty in both the micro and macro realms of the created order. Life only seems to be calm if we stand still at the center of things and don't dare to launch out into the winds that are whirling about just inches away.

Not only is there a whirlwind out there, we also feel stuck in our lives. Where is the direction of things? What is the purpose of all of our busy-ness? There is too much "doing" and not enough "being" in our days. We seem stuck in our jobs, in our relationships, in our politics, and in our faith.

Some believe that we are on the threshold of a new age—a new paradigm shift in science, economics, politics, and in religion. I happen to believe that this is true. There are two popular responses to the idea of radical change. One is hopeful, adventurous and involved; the other is pessimistic, fearful and closed down. You are probably reading this because you favor the prior category. Most of us are in a little of each of these categories, but you probably tend to lean more towards an open and adventurous attitude than to a closed and pessimistic one.

Jonah, was a man who vacillated mightily between these two attitudes. When he failed at his risking he retreated dramatically. One of his deepest retreats was to the belly of a whale. There is great symbolism in Jonah's "stuckness" in the deep watery chaos of the leviathan's belly. Jonah discovered that in his descent into what seemed like hell, the very Source and Power of Life was present—in the midst of the abyss! Jonah is literally spit back into life, reintegrated and differentiated. Once again he goes off on his journey to do great things.

Suffering Job is also an archetypal figure who found himself seriously stuck in the pains of loss and illness. There was no place to go or even hide. His friends just made things worse. Job truly wanted to die. Then came the Whirlwind—that deep metaphor of chaos, danger and promise. The whirlwind is symbolic of God's awe-filling presence. There's no controlling it. All we can do is be present to it, trust it, and ride it.

This section is about learning to ride the Whirlwind of Creation. We are all created differently and mysteriously, and yet there are patterns within patterns that we can get a glimpse of. Yes, the Universe is chaotic, but there is a discernible order behind and underneath that chaos. Most of us call that order God, others may prefer to call it the Mystery of Life, or Life's self-organizing principle. Followers of sacred traditions have long known that it is best not to name the Holy, for the Holy is uncontainable—unnamable.

Christian mystics, and explorers of the human psyche, like Carl Jung, Isabel Myers, and a host of many others have given us some valuable tools that help us to contend and ride life's wild winds, waters, dry deserts and Spirit. As a student of physics, religion, and psychology, I offer this section's way into the desert and whirlwind, as a way for you to jump-start your sacred journey. Come, travel on. I invite you to engage the dragons and the monsters. Be your true and vulnerable self and give yourself to the wonder and vastness of the tempest. The prize of victory and transformation awaits your participation.

I will be inter-mixing a number of metaphors in this section. *Chaotic life* and the *whirlwind* are one and the same, except that when we exercise faith, chaos is transformed into a whirlwind where we experience God. Likewise, *stuck life* and the *desert* are one and the same, except that when we exercise faith, our stuck-ness is transformed into a desert where we encounter God. The desert is an ancient meeting place of the Holy; the whirlwind is a more contemporary metaphor for encountering the Holy, as our lives today are so frenetic. I use both of these metaphors because many contemporary people experience God according to one, the other, or both.

The Desert as Way to a Deeper Experience of God

> It is no whim of history that the birth of the first monotheistic faith took place in a desert....[42]

> And the heavens opened and the Spirit descended upon him like a dove, and a voice came from heaven, 'Thou art my beloved Son; with thee I am well pleased.' The Spirit immediately <u>drove</u> him out into the wilderness. And he was in the wilderness forty days, tempted by Satan; and he was with wild beasts; and the angels ministered to him.
>
> —*Mark 1:10b-13*

Moses led the people of Israel into the desert just as the Spirit drove Jesus into the desert. In each case the journey of the People of God of the Old Testament and of the New Testament was begun. Many followers of God have followed in the way of the desert. Who are some of these fore-bearers into the desert? What was their experience?

Anthony of Egypt (251-356)
Many of the first Christians fled to the desert out of fear of persecution. Anthony is one of the early desert fathers whose motivation was not so much for safety as for purification. The church's tradition of desert spirituality begins with Anthony. Six months after his parent's death, Anthony identifies with Jesus' call to the rich

young man to sell all and give to the poor so that he might have treasure in heaven. Eventually Anthony locks himself in an old fortress for 20 years, "fighting demons," reading Scripture, singing psalms, fasting, and praying. When he finally emerges he is described by Athanasius as "one whose state of soul was purity." "He maintained utter equilibrium, like one guided by reason and steadfast in that which accords with nature."[43]

Gregory of Nyssa (332-395)

Gregory was an early bishop and theologian of the church. In writing <u>The Life of Moses</u>, he describes Moses' experience of God on Mount Sinai as an experience of learning darkness. "When…Moses grew in knowledge, he declared that he had seen God in the darkness, that is, that he had then come to know that what is divine is beyond all knowledge and comprehension, for the text says, 'Moses approached the dark cloud where God was.' What God? He 'who made darkness his hiding place….' Our knowing keeps on penetrating deeper until by intelligence's yearning for understanding it gains access to the invisible and incomprehensible, and there it sees God…this is the seeing that consists in not seeing."[44]

Dionysius the Areopagite (c. 500)

This mystical writer, whose actual identity is unknown to us, spoke like Gregory of Nyssa of finding God in the darkness. "Unto this darkness which is beyond light we pray that we may come, and may attain unto vision through the loss of sight and knowledge, and that in ceasing thus to see or to know understanding (for this emptying of our faculties is true sight and knowledge), and that we may offer Him that transcends all things, the praises of a transcendent hymnody, which we shall do by denying or removing all things that we are."[45]

Julian of Norwhich (1342-1416)

Julian is the first English lay woman whose writings are known to us. Her experience of union with God is focused in her shared experience of crucifixion and suffering with Christ. "When Christ was in pain we were in pain. All creatures of God's creation that can suffer pain suffered with him."[46]

The Frankfurter (c1350)

The anonymous author of <u>Theologia Germanica</u>, "the Frankfurter" discovers the experience of God in the midst of daily life. It is primarily a matter of emptying one's will into God's Eternal Will. "How then does union happen?…a truly pure simple repose in the one Eternal Will of God."[47]

Teresa of Avila (1515-1582)

Considered the founder of the Order of the Discalced Carmelites, Teresa shows a practical balance between head and heart spirituality. She describes her experience of God in the last (7th) "room" of her <u>Interior Castle</u> as follows: "in this temple of God, in this, his own mansion, he and the soul alone rejoice together in supreme silence. The understanding need not stir, nor seek for anything more; the Lord who created it, wishes it now to be at rest."[48]

John of the Cross (1542-1591)

Referred to by some as the "mystic's mystic," John was Teresa's confessor. John is most known for his reference to the experience of the "dark night of the soul." "It is evident that the faith is a dark night of the soul, and it is thus that it gives it light; the more it darkens the soul the more does it enlighten it."[49] "To arrive at being all, desire to be nothing. To come to the knowledge of all, desire the knowledge of nothing."[50]

William Law (1686-1761)

An English non-juror and tutor, Law was known for his austerity and disciplined life style all of which was totally committed to God. Law's <u>Serious Call to a Devout and Holy Life</u> has a lot to say about right behavior. Law's call for all to be humble is a call to the desert of powerlessness. Every person, he says, "must lay aside the opinions and passions which he has received from the world...before he can be governed by the spirit of humility."[51]

Simone Weil (1909-1943)

Weil was a French existentialist who spoke through the ambiguity and emergency of her day. Sometimes called a 'witness to the absolute,' Weil experienced the reality of God in what she called "watchful stillness." "When the soul has once crossed a threshold through a real contact with pure good—of which internal tumult before the sacraments is perhaps a sure sign—nothing further is asked of it except motionless attention."[52]

Thomas Merton (1915-1968)

A Cistercian monk who clearly proclaimed the monastic life to be a prophetic witness over against culture, rather than a withdrawal from the world. Unquestionably, the desert wilderness is for Merton the place where one receives from God a vision for the world. "We do not go to the desert to escape people but to learn to find them; we do not leave them in order to have nothing to do with them, but to find out the way to do them the most good. But this is only a secondary end. The one end that includes all others is the love of God."[53]

Martin Luther King, Jr. (1929-1968)

King's desert was powerlessness and suffering. As he lived through these desert experiences clinging onto a vision of "satyagraha" (love/truth-force) or non-violence, he not only experienced God, but was filled with the power of God that undeniably changed the course American social history. "My personal trials have also taught me the value of unmerited suffering.... I have attempted to see my personal ordeals as an opportunity to transfigure myself and heal the people involved in the tragic situation.... I can now humbly, yet proudly say, 'I bear in my body the marks of the Lord Jesus.... In the past the idea of a personal God was little more than a metaphysical category that I found theologically and philosophically satisfying, now it is a living reality that has been vindicated in the experiences of everyday life.... I have felt the power of God transforming the fatigue of despair into buoyancy of hope...in the struggle for righteousness man has cosmic companionship."[54]

We see in all these witnesses to the presence of God in the desert images and experiences that keep repeating themselves, images and experiences such as darkness, emptiness, nothingness, pain and suffering, silence, struggling and wrestling, powerlessness, and reposing and waiting in the Will of God. The desert is not only the gateway to a journey into God; it also becomes the oasis along the way, and ultimately the place of transfiguration into the "likeness" of God.

The most important point of the idea of the desert is that the desert is a place to experience the living presence of God.

"God himself is the only reason for wanting to enter the desert; desire to see his face is the only motive powerful enough to keep us moving; belief in his power is the only support which can prevent us from falling to pieces; and only the actual experience of his presence gives meaning to our desert spaces.... There is a journey that each of us must take alone.... God has built into us a radical aloneness that only he can fill. It is this journey that I call the desert, and it requires courage to enter the spaces of our interior self where there is no other living being but God.... The call to the desert is the call to deep life.... Many people spend most of their lives resisting this attraction. Some people are driven into the desert by circumstances. It may be prison, a concentration camp, a serious illness, a 'hitting bottom' after years of drugs or sex or the drive for power.... Some people are driven into the desert by the spirit of truth, or poetry, or art, or the desire for the world to change. Some are driven there explicitly by the love of God...or self or others.

"There are a variety of experiences in the desert. There is fear…hunger and thirst…evil spirits…doubts…sin and temptation, lack of trust in God and cowardliness, laziness and self-indulgence…. But these experiences are not the main focus of the desert.

"What I wish to witness to loud and clear is that the center of my own desert experience has been the presence of a Companion who has taken away my radical loneliness…it is in the desert where I have made the fundamental transition from beautiful thoughts about God to the actual experience of God."[55]

I have introduced this section using both the metaphor of the desert and of the whirlwind. Both are biblical and both describe the transformational nature of life. For the rest of this guide, I will be interchanging and mixing these two metaphors, as both metaphors speak to (1) our inability to control our lives by ourselves, and (2) God's presence in the midst of life's "stuck" places.

Entering, Traversing & Coming Out the Other Side of the Desert/Whirlwind

Let me try to describe what a journey into the desert/storm might look and feel like. Words are never sufficient to describe this journey. Some of this description is personal; some of it I have heard in the experience of others; most of it is metaphorical. Others might speak of this journey in a very different way. My description may seem over-dramatic or over-done to you. Hopefully reading this description will bring to mind your own experience of the desert/storm. Experientially, there seems to me to be six stages into and through the desert/storm.

Home

First there is the place from which it all begins. I call that home. It's where my center of gravity is. It's where I want to be most of the time. It's never quite all that it might be, only a shadowy image of what I yearn for. We all lost Eden in the mythical past, and as sojourners on this earth we seek heaven. Scripture offers bookends for this epic journey. We lose Eden in Genesis, and re-vision it in the book of the Revelation of John. Home is Gaia in Greek mythology—a green paradise that is ecologically and organically, exactly as the gods would have it to be. Home is a place of blue sky and it's that little white cottage (or perhaps a larger palace) with the little white fence (or mote) around it. For me it's where my wife shares time with me and where my children and grandchildren come to share their stories and their awe of life. It's where I smell bread baking in the oven and where my friends gather for supper and experience Eucharist. It's a place of peace. It's where God is Present. It's resting under and eating from God's Tree of Life.

Call

But then suddenly, I awaken as from a dream. Someone is calling, or is it the thunder of a gathering storm? A hunger or a thirst invades my attention. Is it a dream of a better world, or an awareness of the brokenness of my present world? Something is out-of-place. It's something like what the new science calls a bifurcation—it's something like the fruit offered to my brother Adam by my sister Eve, who has heard of something more than what seemed to be. Call is different for different people in different circumstances and in different times. It is filled with paradox and irony. This is the stage that I would name as the call, or the "itch" that demands scratching.

Separation

Now things get more complicated, more wrenching. I hate this part. I experience anguish now, or loneliness, or confusion, or lostness, or powerlessness, or a deep unrest. This is a time of leaving and grieving, of letting go of something that seemed so important in the past. The clouds have turned into a heavy rain, I find that I am weeping, or am I in shock? I sometimes get stuck here in denial. I name this the stage of separation.

Obstacles

Now I am actually in the desert or in the midst of the storm's rage. This is a very uncomfortable and unfamiliar place. It is dark and hard to see. There are obstacles everywhere; potholes in the middle of the road, dragons breathing fire at me, hostile adversaries threatening me, and there is an empty feeling in my gut—an awful anxiety that will not go away. I am dis-eased. I am completely out of control, and filled with dread. Sometimes it would seem better to not be at all, than to be here. This is a prison of darkness with no way out. My situation seems hopeless. My sense of perception is distorted; it's as if I am in a house of horrors where mirrors distort my memory of reality. This is the desert: a place of wildness, a wilderness filed with ferocious beasts. This is the eye of the hurricane, where all of the animals and insects have stopped their communications and are awaiting a dreaded fury. In the midst my helplessness, I project fault on just about everyone and everything, except myself. And then it becomes clear: I and only I, am responsible for being here. An awareness of sinfulness begins to dawn, and I confess my complicity. Dante in his time begins to describe a descent into an abyss—he does it in vivid detail, much better than I could ever imagine it. I am aware of my sin and of the Sin of the world. I cry out, "Help! God help me!"

Grace

Four things happen next. I become aware of an intrusion of my unconscious self into my conscious self. There is an ugly clarity of my culpability. Humbled, I am compelled to admit my offense and my offensiveness. I hear a small voice inside trying to ask for help. I let it out. I decide that I want help, and I will ask for it. Oh, sweet surrender! Some distorted part of my ego dies. I know that I am only dust—mere ash. And then it happens. It is always a surprise at the beginning. For some it's a warmth, an acceptance; for others an awareness of Presence. A voice speaks from within (or is outside?) proclaiming an unconditional Love. Amazing Grace! Sometimes gentle, sometimes overwhelmingly powerful. The mist clears, and I see myself in an incredibly crisp new light. I have a purpose. I have gifts that others actually need. Thank you, Lord! Glory is Yours now and always. I praise You, and thank You for the life you have given me to live.

Transformation

I can't wait to get home. Home is somehow different now. It's simpler, and it fits me better. I need to tell someone about what's happened. Will they believe me? Dare I speak of this experience? I see my relationship to many in a different way. Some of my enemies are now potential allies. There is much to do. My God, it's good to be me. Look how blue the sky has become; I swear that the grass has become greener.

The following chart summaries the sacred journey through the desert.

Home (Blue Skies)
Eden: before the call
"GAIA" and the static environment

The Call (The Gathering Clouds)
from within or without a dream
anticipation (excitement & dread)
hunger & thirst, bifurcations, paradox & irony
packing our bags (costs, maps, partners)

Separation (The Initial Downpour)
leaving
grieving
shock, anger, denial, remembering and letting go

Obstacles (The Destructive Force of the Storm)
deserts & wildernesses
silence, the dark Night of the Soul
potholes and rocks, getting lost, accidents
being out of control
adversaries

1. Mortification/Helplessness
2. Scape Goating
3. Sin

Grace (The still & safe Center of the Storm;
The Power of the Spirit)
revelation, epiphany, rescue or help
mountain tops, liberation, "salvation"

1. Intrusion (awareness)
2. Offense (admission)
3. Decision (ask)
4. Death (accept)

Transformation (New Weather Front)
Returning, new sense of self and community
new connectedness, new visions and dreams
anticipation of new journeys, partnership

At this point it is instructive to see how these stages of the sacred journey through the desert were lived out in the history of Israel's pilgrimage to the Promised Land, and in Jesus' life, death and resurrection.

Israel's Journey

Home	Abraham>Isaac>Jacob=Israel (12 Tribes)
Call	Famine > Moses
Separation	The 12 Plagues, The Exodus
Obstacles	The Red Sea, Pharaoh's Army, The Desert, Complaining, The Golden Calf
Grace	Crossing the Red Sea, Manna, Ten Commandments
Transformation	A People who Know their God in history
The Cycle Repeats	Rise and Fall of the Davidic Kingdom - The Exile

The Jesus Journey Cycle

Home	Nazareth
Call	Jesus in the Temple at twelve, Baptism by John
Separation	Sermon at Nazareth -> Rejection, Forty days in the desert
Obstacles	Jealousy & Fear The Temple Hierarchy The Cowardice of the Disciples The Roman Authority The Cross
Grace	The Resurrection
Transformation	Pentecost The Growth of the Early Church
The Cycle Repeats	Every new Generation must appropriate the Story within their own Lives

I have here illustrated the sacred journey of Israel and Jesus over a whole generation or lifespan. Indeed, your life's journey may someday be an epic story to tell as well, making its contribution to salvation history. Practically speaking, most of our journeys take place in shorter periods of days, weeks or months.

It is one thing to have an awareness of the desert journey, it quite another to learn how to navigate in it, and how to dance around the sacred wells of God's Grace, which are always present in the deserts of life. One of the truly great contributions of the desert fathers and of the fourth through eighth century Irish *religieuse* is their description of their dis-eases (sins) and of the spiritual warfare that they fought in the deserts of Egypt, Syria and Ireland. As great warriors against evil, they discovered sacred "medicines" (virtues and spiritual disciplines) to heal their souls' sin-imposed wounds.

Evagrius Ponticus, a desert father who lived from 346 to 399 AD, was the first to list eight categories of "thoughts" that invaded and distorted the monk's solitude as he tried to commune with the mystery of God's Being. These eight "thoughts" were eventually reformulated by John Cassian (another desert father, and later a builder of monastic community in France, whose wisdom became the primary base for the Irish "Penitentials"—the most important documents describing ancient Celtic monastic culture). Gregory the Great, surely building on St. Augustine, changed Cassian's eight great sins (still used in Eastern Orthodox spirituality today) to what in the West have come to be known as the Seven Deadly (or Capital) Sins.

The Irish Penitentials became the manuals of spiritual and pastoral care for the monks and nuns acting as soul friends and confessors to those who came into the sanctuary of their monastic cities. Ian Bradley elaborates,

> "The Irish Penitentials were designed to promote personal growth and development as much as to punish and correct. They prescribed penances for the eight chief vices: gluttony (which covered excessive talking as well as excessive eating and drinking), fornication, avarice (which was taken to include a general lack of regard for others and self-ishness), anger, dejection, languor, vainglory and pride, as well as for a host of other lesser offences. Following Cassian, the principle on which they operated was that of *contraria contrariies sanantur*, contraries are cured by their contraries. Thus the person who has displayed anger has to cultivate meekness, the one who has been guilty of avarice must exercise generosity and the dejected should strive after spiritual joy. In this way, the Penitentials did not provide simply punishments that fitted the crime, but carefully calculated programs to change attitudes and behavior. The negative element must be replaced by a positive one as part of a progression away from sin and towards Christian perfection.... At the heart of the Irish penitential system was the practice of regular private confession and absolution, understood not as mechanical ritual but as a genuine expression of repentance and desire for *metanoia* or change.[56]

As I considered the importance on the Eight Great Sins and their corresponding virtues as spiritual medicine, and as diagnostic devices for spiritual maturity; I noticed how closely their descriptions fit with the descriptions of the four gateways to the desert that we have previously described.

Even more interesting is the fit that takes place when you expand the four mental functions or "soul languages" (N, S, T and F) on page 47 to their introverted and extroverted counterparts (N_e & N_i, S_e & S_i, T_e & T_i, F_e & F_i). I have named these eight categories, the "Eight Deserts" of the spiritual journey.

The following two pages of charts integrates these Eight Deserts with the Eight Great Sins, and proposed "treatments" or virtues which can act as wells of Grace in the midst of our spiritual deserts. I have used these eight deserts and wells for two and three day retreats over the past ten years and have found them to accurately describe the experiences that most of us have in the desert.

The Classical Vices of Christendom compared to Jungian "Spiritual Deserts"

	Desert Name and Experiences in the desert	Dominant Function, MBTI type And GIFT	Tendency to Overcome	Inferior Function (Weakest function tries to take over)	Vice Tendencies in the Desert	Virtue(s) To cultivate for growth	Biblical Character as Prototype	Abba Evagrius' original list of the "Eight Thoughts"[1] (c.375 AD)	Eastern Orthodox list of the Eight Passions from Orthodox Spirituality[2]	The Seven Deadly Sins of the West (Rewriting of Evagrius of Ponticus (346-399 AD) work by Gregory the Great, & then again by Thomas Aquinas)[3]
1	**NONSENSE** 1. Physical Collapse & focus on the body. 2. Faulty perception & obsession with "facts." 3. Withdrawal & depression.	**N$_e$** Extroverted Intuition ENTP/ENFP **FAITH**	Excessive Commitment	**S$_i$** Introverted Sensing	Gluttony, Impurity, Drunkenness, Greediness, Extravagance, Ostentation, Intemperance, Excess	Continence, Fasting, Moderation.	Paul	**Gluttony**[4] (Excessive talking as well as eating & drinking) "first thought"[5]	**Gluttony** (gastrimargia)	**Gluttony** (Excessive dependence on food, drink, data, gadgets) *Substituting stuff for God.*
2	**BOUNDARY-LESSNESS** 1. Obsessiveness with external details. 2. Sensual overindulgence. 3. Adversarial role to the world.	**N$_i$** Introverted Intuition INFJ/INTJ **HOPE**	Excessive Vision and Goals	**S$_e$** Extroverted Sensing	Impurity, Gluttony, Obscenity, Incest, Pornography, Adultery, Lewdness	Chastity, Self-Control, Continence.	Joseph son of Jacob	**Fornication** "second thought"	**Impurity** (porneia)	**Lust** *Substituting others for God*
3	**CONFUSED VISION** 1. Internal confusion. 2. Inappropriate understanding. 3. Grandiose visions.	**S$_e$** Extroverted Sensing ESTP/ESFP **COURAGE**	Excessive Activity and Power	**N$_i$** Introverted Intuition	Pride, Vanity, Boasting, Insubordination, Presumption, Disobedience, Flippancy, Hypocrisy, Ambition	Obedience, Humility, Awe & Wonder.	Peter	**Pride** "eighth thought"	**Vainglory** (kenodoxia)	**Pride** *Substituting self for God*
4	**INCOMPETENCE** 1. Loss of control over facts and details. 2. Impulsiveness. 3. Catastrophizing.	**S$_i$** Introverted Sensing ISTJ/ISFJ **DUTY**	Excessive Duty	**N$_e$** Extroverted Intuition	Sloth, Melancholy, Cynicism, Laziness, Trepidation, Neglect, Imprudence	Zeal, Courage, Perseverance, Cheerfulness. Penthos or mourning	Martha	**Despondency (Languor)** "sixth thought"	**Melancholy** (Lupe)	**Sloth** (Acedia) *Substituting nothing for God*

#	Type	Function	Excessive	Function	Vices / Tendencies	Virtue	Biblical Figure	Thought	Greek Term	Sin
5	**MEANINGLESSNESS** 1. Excessive criticism of others. 2. Compulsive search for exacting truth. 3. Distorted logic.	**F_e** Extroverted Feeling ESFJ/ENFJ **LOVE**	Excessive Connectedness	**T_i** Introverted Thinking	Jealous, Envy, Vain, Slander, defamation, ridicule, disunity, hatred, accusation	Spiritual Joy.	John the Apostle	Dejection "fifth thought"	Slander (katalalia)	**Envy or Jealousy** *Substituting others for God*
6	**TRUSTLESSNESS** 1. Focus on incompetence. 2. Hypersensitive to signs of dishonesty. 3. Take precipitous action to correct imagined error.	**F_i** Introverted Feeling ISFP/INFP **EMPATHY**	Excessive Valuing	**T_e** Extroverted Thinking	Anger, Irascibility, Fearfulness, Hatred, Fury, Disunity, Injury, Impatience, Self-Love	Meekness, Patience,	Mary the mother of Jesus	Anger "fourth thought"	Irascibility (orge or oxycholia)	**Anger** *Substituting self for God*
7	**POWERLESSNESS** 1. Hypersensitive to relationship issues. 2. Outbursts of extreme emotion. 3. Fear of feeling.	**T_e** Extroverted Thinking ESTJ/ENTJ **ADMINISTRATION**	Excessive Control	**F_i** Introverted Feeling	Dejection, bitterness, Opinionated, Bossy, vanity	Connecting with others	Nehemiah	Vainglory "seventh thought"	Bitterness (pikria)	X
8	**LONELINESS** 1. Touchy and emotional. 2. Hypersensitive to relationship issues. 3. Overemphasized logic.	**T_i** Introverted Thinking ISTP/INTP **PLANNING**	Excessive Objectivity	**F_e** Extroverted Feeling	Covetous, Acquisitive, Greedy, Materialistic, Self-indulgence, Usury, Theft	Generosity, Alms Giving,	Matthew	Avarice "third thought" (Taken to include a general lack of regard for others and selfishness)	Covetousness (phylargyria)	**Covetousness** *Substituting stuff for God*

1. This list was modified by John Cassian, whose Marseilles community probably carried his writings to Ireland where they were adapted in the Irish Penitentials (the single largest group of documents to have survived the golden age of Celtic Christianity).

2. Anonymous Monk of the Eastern Church, Orthodox Spirituality: An Outline of the Orthodox Ascetical and Mystical Tradition (SVS Press, 1978) pp. 51-52.

3. St. Augustine probably encouraged the first western rewrite which made pride the chief sin and combined dejection with acedia, while introducing envy. In the 12c. Aquinas combined pride with vainglory.

4. Note that Gluttony and Lust are companion deserts, sharing the same inferior function, and are thus shaded together in the chart - as are all of the companion desert pairs. The desert pairs will often have vice/virtue tendencies cross over from one to the other.

5. Evagrius arranged his thoughts in order, beginning with the monk's first challenge in his desert hut and proceeding to the next. Cassian reversed the order of Dejection with Anger.

The battles that we fight in our spiritual deserts are often matters of life and death, where we sometimes come out the other end of the experience changed, transformed into that person that God wants us to be. There is no necessary pattern or rhythm to these episodes that corresponds to our age or our physical and emotional development. They can happen at any time, at any place, and at any age.

Classical Christian spiritualities in the West and in the East have each spoken of three dynamics or phases within the process of the soul's development. The categories speak of a time of purgation or trial which leads to a time of illumination and understanding, which in turn leads to a time of unity when one experiences a new connectedness to God and to God's creation.

> "Under different names these classifications generally recur, and they contain a nucleus of truth. But none has an absolute value. The various states penetrate each other. The soul rises and falls back from one to the other without following any rule. Moreover these classifications express states of the soul rather than the objective data of God's action. They mark some moments of our own human existence rather than moments of the life of the Saviour. They are anthropocentric rather than theocentric.[57]

The next section of this paper will look at the "theocentric" stages of the soul's progress through life.

Exercises:

1. Review the chart of the Eight Deserts. Can you find which desert tends to fit your life experiences best? If not, pick one that looks like it might be close to your life experience. **Appendix C** at the end of this guide describes each of the eight deserts in greater detail (the destructive forces as well as the "amazing" experiences of Grace).

    Now try to discern if there is a particular pattern of failure, or vice, or temptation, or life situation to which you are particularly vulnerable. Name it, and describe it in writing (journal) as best as you can.

    Next, (this is important), try to recall if there has been a way that you have been able to willfully summon or evoke a virtue, or a positive behavior, or an attitude that has put you in a place where your desert suddenly became more tolerable, or where you suddenly have found your self warmed by God's Presence or surprised by God's Grace. If you are able to name such a virtue, behavior or attitude, describe it in as much detail as you can and tuck that information away for future use next time you find yourself in a spiritual desert.

2. Utilizing the terminology that we have introduced in this section, do some journaling on an experience of going through a recent desert (or storm).

My Desert/Storm Journey:

"Home" (What was good about your life, before this desert/storm experience)	
My Call (Where did the trigger or the pull towards the desert/storm come from?)	
My Separations (Tears, Mourning, Leavings, Pain, Denials)	
Obstacles (Sins, Vices, Traps)	
God's Grace (Virtues, Wells of Grace)	
My Transformation (How were you changed?)	
The Cycle Repeats (What's different about "Home" after your return?)	

Following are examples of Wells of Grace, or of Triggers of Nurture in the Desert. (Note that Grace can never be forced or manipulated. It is a free gift. It is always available. The barriers to it are of our own making. In "dancing" around potential wells of Grace, we make ourselves available to the infinitely rich medicine of God's healing Grace.)

The practice of particular virtues, physical exercise, rest, sleep, dreams, humor, engaging in a hobby, meditation, contemplation, active prayer, service, confession, time with a spiritual director or soul friend, reading the Scriptures, reading from spiritual mentors, receiving sacraments (esp. Eucharist, Unction), laying on of hands, singing, holy conversation, listening to others, listening to nature, theatre, movies, walking, journaling, saying the Jesus prayer or other mantra, pilgrimage, time in the mountains, or by the water, time in solitude.

Section Six

The Three Conversions:
Necessary Pilgrimages for the
Soul-Journeyer

...would it be possible to discover an itinerary of spiritual life...
emphasizing the divine operation rather than the psychology on the
soul in **via***?...Nicholas Cabasilas shows us where the scale of the*
degrees is to be found. He distinguishes three essential moments in
spiritual life: Baptism, Chrism (confirmation by unction),
Eucharist.... The three holy mysteries of Baptism, Chrisma and
Eucharist are the three essential stages in the way that leads to God.[58]
—an anonymous monk of
the Eastern Orthodox Church

So far we have spoken of four practices or opportunities to advance into a healthier and livelier spiritual life; namely, (1) repentance or tears and confession, (2) balancing attention on the inner and outer life, (3) discovering which of the four soul languages or types (with its gateways to God) fits your God given identity, and finally (4) discerning your journey strategies for spiritual warfare in the desert along with the "medicines" or wells of grace to refresh your soul in battle.

All of these practices are useful for all the seasons of one's life. Now I would like to turn to looking at the long view of your life's spiritual journey. Is there a way of discovering and evaluating where you are in answering the call that God has given you to live out your life in this world as a child of Creation, sharing in the discipleship of the Incarnate One, empowered by the Grace and the Breath of God's life giving Spirit? Are there stages of conversion, and rituals and covenants to mark the way that coincides with the stages of our physical, socio-political, and psychological growth?

The Church's answer through the ages has been a resounding, "Yes," though we seem of late to have lost a sense of the importance of these ascending spiritual graces. Our present "enlightened" culture has offered a number of interesting and often helpful psychologically based substitutes, but we are coming now to painfully learn that no human evolved science can ever substitute itself for the Love and Grace of the Living God. In this section we will move from our past emphasis on human nature to an emphasis on divine action.

There are of course dangers in seeing ourselves as progressing into "greater" stages of holiness. Is it ever helpful or even really meaningful to see oneself as "further along" in God's Way than your neighbor? Let us proclaim a loud and final "No" to that temptation—for it is just that—a temptation to give into pride, vainglory, and avarice. We are all perfect creations in the Creator's Eye. We are all wonderfully unique and incomparable to one another in terms of our final worth. To compare the glory of gold to that of silver, ultimately is a waste of time, even if one is worth more than the other according to some economic indicator, artificially created by the world's sense of supply and demand. In the end we are each only in competition with ourselves. God has uniquely destined each of us for an end. It is our life's work to discern that end and live it out. No one can do that for us, and no one is called to the same vocation, so comparisons are futile. On the other hand, we can learn from the good and the heroic in others' giving of their lives to the world's great need. To learn from one another is a far different thing than to be jealous of another's contribution or of their giftedness. We all suffer from the temptations of avarice or jealousy, and the world is a far worse place because of this wasted and near-sighted use of creative energy.

The three stages of spiritual growth coincide with the experiences of (1) *community* which encourages the discernment of personal identity, (2) *conversation* which encourages the discernment of social vocation, and (3) *commitment* which encourages the giving of one's life (and therefore one's final, singular and unique death) to the cause of healing the earth (a part of God's great cosmos) of its brokenness. Notice that there is a progression here from the personal to the social to the cosmic. The journey outward into the cosmos, leads inward to a growth of the soul working cooperatively with the Divine Will. These three stages also (thanks to the genius of the church's sacramental practice) coincide perfectly with the Grace bestowing rituals of Baptism, Confirmation/Reaffirmation, and Eucharist.

While these three stages of pilgrimage are consecutive, each stage remains ongoing throughout one's life. That is to say we never complete the journey into our identity (first stage), and our identity is further transformed as we engage in the work of vocation (second stage) and the work of the acceptance of our death (third stage).

The following chart begins to integrate these various episodes of spiritual pilgrimage:

Three Life Stages of the Soul's Conversion to Christ

	First Conversion	Second Conversion	Third Conversion
Realm:	Personal	Social	Cosmic
Conversion of the:	Heart	Heart & Mind	Heart, Mind & Will
Context:	Community	Conversation	Commitment
Sacrament:	Baptism	Chrism: Confirmation and/or Reaffirmation	Eucharist
The essential Love (gift of God) that is experienced:	*Storge* (natural parental love)	*Phillipe* (natural brotherly love) & *Eros* (natural erotic love)	*Agape* (love that is supernatural, requiring an act of the will)
Sign:	Promise	Covenant	Transformation
Experience:	Incorporation, Hospitality	Gift Awareness, Vocational Experimentation	Death, Hope for the Future, Reconciliation
Relationship to God:	As a child of God	As a brother to Jesus	As one in union with the Triune One
Wisdom Figure:	John the Apostle	Paul the Theologian	Peter the Martyr
Overcoming:	The Ego and False Identity	Ignorance and Fear	Death
To Discover:	True Identity	True Vocation	Life's Ultimate Purpose

Years ago, when Jay Hanson and I did our first "deserts and wells" retreat for about fifty communicants of St. John the Evangelist Episcopal Church in St. Paul, Minnesota, we were responding to the Rector and a spirituality committee of the congregation who expressed a desire to retreat from the entrapments of their busy and often unproductive lives. The Rector was also keen to explore the meaning of Jesus' teaching that all who hold on to their lives will lose them, but those who are willing to let go of their lives for Jesus' sake and for the sake of the Kingdom will find their lives forever.

Indeed, there is a strong connection between this teaching of Jesus (found in some form in all four of the Gospels) and the conversion of the soul through the three stages mentioned above. I would like to suggest that this teaching of Jesus is central to the Gospel. To understand this teaching and to live it is paramount to becoming a productive and authentic Christian disciple.

Let's look now at the three stages of the soul's conversion, one by one, through the lens of Jesus' teaching in Matthew 16:24—17:13.

> Then Jesus told his disciples, "If any want to become my followers, let them deny themselves and take up their cross and follow me. For those who want to save their life will lose it, and those who lose their life for my sake will find it. For what will it profit them if they gain the whole world but forfeit their life? Or what will they give in return for their life? For the Son of Man is to come with his angels in the glory of his Father, and then he will repay everyone for what has been done. Truly I tell you, there are some standing here who will not taste death before they see the Son of Man coming in his kingdom."
>
> Six days later, Jesus took with him Peter and James and his brother John and led them up a high mountain, by themselves. And he was transfigured before them, and his face shone like the sun, and his clothes became dazzling white. Suddenly there appeared to them Moses and Elijah, talking with him. Then Peter said to Jesus, "Lord, it is good for us to be here; if you wish, I will make three dwellings here, one for you, one for Moses, and one for Elijah." While he was still speaking, suddenly a bright cloud overshadowed them, and from the cloud a voice said, "This is my Son, the Beloved; with him I am well pleased; listen to him!" When the disciples heard this, they fell to the ground and were overcome by fear. But Jesus came and touched them, saying, "Get up and do not be afraid."
>
> And when they looked up, they saw no one except Jesus himself alone. As they were coming down the mountain, Jesus ordered them, "Tell no one about the vision until after the Son of Man has been raised from the dead." And the disciples asked him, "Why, then, do the scribes say that Elijah must come first?" He replied, "Elijah is indeed coming and will restore all things; but I tell you that Elijah has already come, and they did not recognize him, but they did to him whatever they pleased. So also the Son of Man is about to suffer at their hands." Then the disciples understood that he was speaking to them about John the Baptist.

Stage One: The Conversion of the Heart, Consummated in Community through Baptism

> Then Jesus told his disciples, "If any want to become my followers, let them deny themselves and take up their cross and follow me. For those who want to save their life will lose it, and those who lose their life for my sake will find it. For what will it profit them if they gain the whole world but forfeit their life? Or what will they give in return for their life? For the Son of Man is to come with his angels in the glory of his Father, and then he will repay everyone for what has been done."
>
> —*Matthew 16:24-27*

Jesus' private conversation here with his disciples at Caesarea Philippi takes place just as he is finishing his three years of public ministry. Jesus has gone up as far north as he ever goes, near the foot of Mount Hermon. He now turns his head towards Jerusalem, and begins the long march to the Holy City which ultimately leads to his crucifixion and resurrection. This is a moment of summing up his earthly ministry with his students, who will soon be commissioned to carry on the incarnate ministry of salvation that Jesus has initiated for all time. Jesus is speaking to his followers at a very crucial moment. Will the disciples understand?

I did not really understand this teaching until I was in college in the 1960's, at the University of Wisconsin in Madison—a very secular university where I was preparing to become an engineer. My baptism had taken place seventeen years earlier, but I still didn't get what Jesus was asking of us in the Gospel. A yearning deep inside of me led me to leave the engineering campus for one course in one of the liberal arts buildings where there was a three credit offering being taught on the great teachers of the Christian Way. Incredibly in that class a Christian believer challenged us to understand the meaning and application of Matthew 16:25. I learned that to live was to die, and to die was to live. "In baptism we die with Christ in his crucifixion, so that we might live with him in his resurrection" (Book of Common Prayer, The Sacrament of Holy Baptism, page 306). Authentic living (a very important concept to me then) had something to do with my willingness to accept my own death.

This was a time in my life when I was desperately trying to figure out who I was. I was trying hard to be something that I thought would be really significant, something that would fit in with what my world saw as prestigious and important. To that end I joined a fraternity. It was in that community (also very secular) that I learned how to let my false ego die a much needed death. In those days you had to go through an abominable "rush" period where your loyalties to the brothers were tested by challenges of staying up all night, wearing odorous sack cloth underneath your clothes, and running meaningless errands. My sense of dignity and importance rebelled against these demands.

At the "kangaroo court" in the inner sanctum of the fraternity's bar, a spot light was turned on each pledge in turn (I was saved for last) to receive the judgment of the brothers. Were we in, or were we out? When my turn came, I heard just what these "new friends" really thought of me. They focused on my rebellious and uncooperative temperament. My ego was demolished. Horror of horrors, big old tough me broke down in tears. That night as I walked the streets of Madison, ending up in the chapel of the campus' Episcopal Student Center where I lived, I prayed for help. On that night a very false part of me died, and a new identity began to emerge. Wonder of wonders, the fraternity did take me in—but it was a different me they came to know. More importantly, I changed my major from engineering to physics and took all of the rest of course work at the liberal arts campus.

It was at this moment in my life that I realized how important my parents were, and how influential all of my years in Christian community had been. My mentors now became my college chaplain and my home town priest. The hospitality of my parents, my fellowships of Christian friends had slowly and patiently, all those early years of my life, introduced me to the Living Christ. Miracle upon miracle, I began to hear Christ call my name, and the voice of the One who named me said, "You are my friend, and you are loved", and I knew that I was; I was becoming all I needed to be.

This is part of the story of the conversion of my heart. This "first" conversion of the baptismal experience is still in process. We are all works in progress. All of the three conversions to Christ intermingle in life. But a point was reached finally in my life which enabled me now to listen more deeply to the conversation that would in time lead to the beginning of my second conversion, the conversion of my mind.

Before moving on to the second conversion of the Christian spiritual journey, let me summarize what I understand to be the essential gifts of the first grace of Baptism:

(1) The gift of a Name, which is the gift of identity. In Baptism the false ego begins to die (to drown) in the waters of baptism. We begin to look in the mirror and see that our face is becoming the face of Christ. We are moving from "glory to glory" in our incorporation into Christ's Body.

(2) The gift of Christian community. We can never discover our true self by our self. It is only in a loving and accepting community of faith that our true self is revealed to us. It is a wonder to discover that community in just about any place in the world. Even in "secular" places such as fraternities and university classrooms, the incarnate humanity of the Christ can manifest itself.

(3) The promise of eternal life is introduced to us in Baptism. In dying we begin to understand that a greater life becomes possible. The door to that new life begins to become visible to us. We will still need to walk finally through it in the stage of the third conversion.

(4) In baptism we told that our future vocation is tied up in Jesus' vocation. The whole congregation says in our baptismal liturgy:

"We receive you into the household of God. Confess the faith of Christ crucified, proclaim his resurrection, and share with us in his eternal priesthood." (Book of Common Prayer, p. 308)

It is within this hospitality of the community of the faith that we discover the depths of the Love that God has for us, and living in that Love we are given permission to repent of our false strivings and self serving ways. In the Love of that community we are forgiven and healed. We live into our Baptismal identity and we discover that that identity is very, very good.

Stage Two: The Conversion of the Mind, Consummated in Conversation through Confirmation and Reaffirmation

Six days later, Jesus took with him Peter and James and his brother John and led them up a high mountain, by themselves. And he was transfigured before them, and his face shone like the sun, and his clothes became dazzling white. Suddenly there appeared to them Moses and Elijah, talking with him. Then Peter said to Jesus, "Lord, it is good for us to be here; if you wish, I will make three dwellings here, one for you, one for Moses, and one for Elijah." While he was still speaking, suddenly a bright cloud overshadowed them, and from the cloud a voice said, "This is my Son, the Beloved; with him I am well pleased; listen to him!" When the disciples heard this, they fell to the ground and were overcome by fear. But Jesus came and touched them, saying, "Get up and do not be afraid." And when they looked up, they saw no one except Jesus himself alone.

—Matthew 17:1-8

Peter, James and John are Jesus' best students. He invites them away for a kind of weekend retreat to prepare them for leadership roles in the Church that is to evolve after Pentecost. They do not know yet what those leadership roles are to be or even that such a thing as a Church is going to form. These three are all very different from one another. John will eventually becomes a kind of patron saint for Eastern Orthodoxy as well as for Celtic Christianity—whose character will come to emphasize the inner spiritual life. Peter becomes the Rock, the head of the Western Church—who will come to be characterized as emphasizing the external order of the Church. Finally James, John's brother, son of Zebedee, was the first of the twelve to be martyred (Acts 12:2). His execution (about A.D. 44), by order of King Herod Agrippa I of Judea, was part of a larger persecution in which Peter was arrested (Acts 12:1-3). Each of these great Church leaders was different; each had to discover his unique vocational call.

During these past three years Jesus has become more then a charismatic prophet and rabbi to them; he has also become their mentor and their friend. The three disciples are now listening to their mentor in conversation with Moses and Elijah, two of the greatest of figures in their holy tradition. I would love to know what they said, what lessons they taught. Luke 9:31 gives a hint: "They [Moses and Elijah] appeared in glory and were speaking of his departure, which he was about to accomplish at Jerusalem."

Some time must have passed before Peter offers to build a more comfortable environment for their retreat house on the holy mountain. Already Peter is showing signs that he is a builder. At that precise moment a bright cloud overshadows them and the voice of God is heard to say, "This is my Son, the Beloved; with whom I am well pleased; listen to him." These are the same words spoken about Jesus at his baptism. This is a time when Jesus' true Messianic vocation is being revealed to the three leaders in the making. "Listen to him!" This is a time for instruction and understanding, a time for them to begin testing their vocations. They need to get used to the Mystery, for it is that Mystery that will kindle their imaginations and give them the strength they will need to lead. But, they do not understand, and they are overcome with fear. Then Jesus does what he has so often done before, he comes to them and touches them, diminishing their fear so that they continue to grow in their understanding.

The second conversion that the disciples must experience in their life's journey is the conversion of their minds which will lead to an awareness of their call. It is one thing to personally know that you are Loved and that you have a unique identity (Baptism); it is quite another to know that you have a purpose—a service to render (Confirmation). This is about moving from the personal to the social order of life. The second conversion is a conversion to the church. It is a conversion which takes seriously that we are called by God to serve on behalf of our community of formation; the community that will continue to sustain and nurture. But now that nurture is for vocation and service, not for just identity. In the community of faith, there is a whole range of saints, including its Moses and

Elijahs who instruct and form the mind. This is a time of gift discernment. In Baptism the gifts of the Spirit are introduced, now in Confirmation they are embodied. In the act of Confirmation, the bishop lays their hands on the confirmand's head and says,

> "Strengthen O Lord your servant *N.* with your Holy Spirit; empower *him* for your service, and sustain *him* all the days of *his* life." (Book of Common Prayer, p. 418)

The second conversion is about being empowered for service, for which we need God's strength and sustenance.

The reason that I transferred out of the school of engineering to the school of liberal arts was that I came to realize that the particular gifts that God had given to me had more to do with people than with structures. What a great discovery this was for me. As much as I loved the idea of discovering the mysteries of the universe, what I was finding more compelling was the flesh and blood mystery of our humanity. This discovery took time. I had to experiment successfully and unsuccessfully with relationships. Every day became an experiment. I was the experiment. The laboratory was made up of my friends and teachers and mentors. I often stayed up into the depths of the night talking about God with my house mates at St. Frances House, the Campus Episcopal Center where I resided. We talked about Thomas Aquinas' "proofs" of the existence of God, about the meaning of death, about what our futures might be like, and on and on. Three of my house brothers and I eventually sought Holy Orders and were ordained. Who would have thought that would happen to any of us? It was a surprise to many of our families and friends. I remember and cherish the exploratory conversations I had with our University chaplain, Gerald White, and my hometown parish priest, Vic Bolle. Their wisdom and patience gave me space and permission to pray and to listen, and finally to discern a call to priesthood. I had been confirmed nine years before my ordination time came around. My second conversion took a great deal of time, and kept getting refined in my decision to marry and in my acceptance of a call to the episcopate.

Like Baptism, Confirmation and Reaffirmation never stop. They are conversion processes that continue to frame and mold us into the likeness of Jesus, who we come to know as both our brother and our mentor. But it is clear that Baptism must precede Confirmation. Identity forms the base out of which vocation is birthed. And vocation provides the base out of which living the Paschal or Eucharistic life emerges.

A word needs to be said about the Episcopal Church's present practice of Confirmation. In our earlier prayer books, Confirmation was understood to be done at about age twelve, and it was essentially a prerequisite for the reception of

Holy Communion. The 1979 Book of Common Prayer has given a much needed focus on the importance of baptismal initiation. Baptism now constitutes a full sense of membership in the Body of Christ. This new emphasis on the primacy of the baptismal covenant has opened up the church's need to practice the ministry of all the baptized. Confirmation generally now takes place at age sixteen or later, and is often done regionally, rather than in the local congregation—to emphasize that the confirmand is being commissioned to a vocational ministry that now goes beyond the confines of the local congregation into the world.

Unfortunately, many congregations, and some dioceses have disvalued the importance of Confirmation, assuming that Baptism—properly understood and practiced—gave to the new initiate all that was necessary for their Christian journey; recognizing that there would be many rites of passage (first driver's license, school graduations, new jobs, etc.) as one grew in their faith that would take the place of what was once understood to be Confirmation. The new sacramental opportunity, called Reaffirmation, appropriately contributes to the understanding that our Christian journey has many opportunities where we need to reaffirm our vocational decisions.

It is heartening to note that there is again a growing resurgence in re-appropriating the place and importance of Confirmation as the candidate's initial conversion to Christian vocation. In the normative Christian journey, beginning with infant baptism within the community of faith, Confirmation appropriately marks the conclusion of the initial formation process in the community of faith—just at the a time when young people graduate from high school and contemplate the next stage of their life's vocation. It is well that Confirmation now seriously marks the beginning of the vocational journey, rather then simply allowing one to receive Communion, which rightfully should occur after baptism.

Stage Three: The Conversion of the Will, Consummated in Commitment through Eucharist

As they were coming down the mountain, Jesus ordered them, "Tell no one about the vision until after the Son of Man has been raised from the dead." And the disciples asked him, "Why, then, do the scribes say that Elijah must come first?" He replied, "Elijah is indeed coming and will restore all things; but I tell you that Elijah has already come, and they did not recognize him, but they did to him whatever they pleased. So also the Son of Man is about to suffer at their hands." Then the disciples understood that he was speaking to them about John the Baptist.

—*Matthew 17: 9-13*

Peter, James and John make a connection as they are being prepared for leadership roles. The three disciples understand that when Jesus talked about no one recognizing the return of Elijah, he was referring to John the Baptist. What they don't get is that the Baptist's connection to Elijah was that as Elijah had to give way to Elisha, so too John gives way to Jesus. Jesus is talking about transitions—his and ultimately theirs. The three also still do not understand that Jesus' reference to the Son of Man's impending suffering at the hands of those who killed the Baptist is a reference to Jesus' coming crucifixion. But the thing that is most personally terrifying and as yet not known to the three, is that these great leaders of the early church must each suffer a kind of martyrdom themselves before their life journey and final conversion to Christ's likeness is complete. Their martyrdoms will all be different. Peter, like Jesus, will suffer crucifixion, John will suffer exile, and James will be killed in Jerusalem. All three, in the end, willingly accept their death as a part of their life's destiny and meaning. The sharing of Christ's death spoken of in Baptism finally comes full circle in their respective martyrdoms.

Jesus, Elijah and the Baptist are known by their suffering and by their martyrdom. Martyrdom then becomes the most recognizable sign of Christian identity. Certainly, the cross is the single most recognizable sign of the Christian faith. Jesus begins his conversation with the three disciples coming down the mountain, by saying, "tell no one about the vision until after the Son of Man has been raised from the dead." The point here is that these three new leaders are the ones that Jesus is calling to explain to the world the connection between martyrdom and Messiahship. They will do this as they accept their calls to discipleship, and live their lives fully to their deaths, never shirking what lies ahead.

This is a hard teaching. The third conversion is about giving your life away for the sake of the world's redemption. The Eucharist is a drama of Jesus' life that is meant to become a drama of our own lives. In receiving the Body and Blood, we are saying "Yes" to having the Christ Life in us, so that our life may be in Christ. The price of this Divine reception is our death. There are three levels to the Eucharistic drama.

At the first level there is the bread and wine which is:
(1) taken, (2) blessed, (3) broken and poured out, and then finally it is (4) given away to be consumed.

The second level is a re-creation of Jesus' life in his:
(1) incarnation and offering of his Divinity to receive humanity, (2) Jesus' baptism and commitment to offer himself for the world's at-one-ment, (3) his crucifixion, and (4) his promise to come again through others and at the "last day."

Then there is the third level that foretells and invites the drama of our own lives into Jesus' life:
(1) our Baptism, (2) our Confirmation, (3) our Martyrdom, and (4) the memory of our sainthood living on in the memory of our children and in the memory of the Church.

The Eastern Orthodox understanding of Eucharist is most instructive:

> Eucharistic grace fulfills the grace of Baptism and Charisma [Confirmation & Reaffirmation]. We may call the grace of Eucharist, "Easter grace," for "Christ our Passover is sacrificed for us" (1 Cor. 5:7). In the Paschal mystery—The Holy of Holies—we find the three essential aspects or moments of the Eucharist: The Lord's Supper, the Passion and the Resurrection. Only a distorted piety can separate the Upper Room from Golgotha and the Sepulcher. The three sacred days—*triduum sacrum*, as the Latin liturgical books say—constitute an indivisible whole. There is but one Passover.[59]

Early in my ministry as a parish priest in the 1960's I began to accept in my head the idea that a willing acceptance of our mortality was a necessary act in our life's pilgrimage. This acceptance is essential if we are ever going to seriously engage in fighting the world's forces of darkness and allow God's reconciling Grace to heal its deep wounds. I saw this especially in the work of anti-racism that I found myself drawn into. Martin Luther King, Jr. and Mahatma Gandhi became my greatest heroes and (distant) mentors. Their willing acceptance of their martyrdom and death left a lasting mark on my social and spiritual consciousness.

My pastoral ministry was influenced by the awareness that death must eventually be accepted if we are to have a peaceful transition to our glory. I would wait for the right moment to sensitively bring up the subject of death with hospital patients who were clearly going to die due to the challenges of a terminal disease. In one particular situation I was severely reprimanded by my superior for having "depressed" a congregant with "thoughts of death" in the weeks just before her "passing away." Undoubtedly, I have not always listened sensitively enough to know the right moment to say the right thing. But, what a tragedy to have one spend their whole life without ever coming to an awareness of the great value that death plays in giving meaning to earthly life and to life everlasting. The meaning of the cross and the naming of Jesus' death day as "Good Friday" are absolutely basic to the Christian story and to the Christian meaning of life. Priests whose vocation is essentially one of "meaning giving" (as Rabbis) often will tell you that Lent and Good Friday are their most looked forward to times of the year. They will also tell you that their ministry in working with the dying, in working with the families of the deceased at the time of death, and in being centrally involved in the funeral liturgy are all some of the most significant occasions of their priestly ministry.

Now that I am past my 65th birthday, the subject of a possible retirement time occasionally arises with my wife at our supper table, or at times when there is extra stress in our lives. We ask, "What does it mean to retire?" We seem to have great difficulty in answering that question. We know that it does not mean going off to some ethereal pasture just to eat, sleep and be "content." But, what does it mean? If it means doing what we always wanted to do, we are perplexed because we are already doing what we believe God wants us to do and we are mostly at peace with that, as we find joy in our ministries. Another question that we ask each other is, "Where should we retire?" Again, wisdom seems to be on a holiday. This question becomes all the more relevant when we find many of our life long friends retiring and asking us about our plans for you know what. I believe that the subject of retirement may be difficult for me to manage because it is essentially a question about my mortality.

The ancient Celtic monks and nuns of Ireland had an intriguing question that they would put to the recipients of their soul friendship. They would ask, "Where will be the place of your resurrection?" In other words, "What 'thin' place or 'edge' place do you want to be at the time of your death, where heaven and earth are close to one another?" The question also is asking, "Where are you most at *home*?"

Remember our discussion about the first stage of the desert journey? I think I can begin to get my imagination around this Celtic question. St. Cuthbert wanted to go to his hermitage as his place of resurrection—and he did, but after his death his monks brought his body back to the Abbey at Lindisfarne which was actually not far from his hermitage. For the Celtic *religiouse,* the monastic city was usually not that far from their favorite place of pilgrimage or their favorite place of solitude. The point of this for me is that my life isn't over until it's over; or my soul cannot begin to conceive of a place of rest until it has discerned its place of, and cause for martyrdom.

Marcus Losack, an Anglican priest of the Church of Ireland, who offers structured Celtic pilgrimages to Glendalough (his own place of residence which is an ancient monastic city) had one final thing to say to me as my wife Ira and I left Glendalough. Looking me straight in the eye he shared the story of St. Kevin, the founder of Glendalough, who in his later years was also thinking about all the pilgrimages he might still make in his life. A stranger appeared to him and simply advised, "Stay in one place." And that is what he did. Marcus looked at me and felt compelled to say, "Ed, stay in one place." And so I wrestle with my mortality and my acceptance of martyrdom, as do we all.

Dying to the Past, We are Reborn to the Future

The first conversion required of us on our way from "glory to glory" into the fullness of Christ (2 Cor. 3:18) *is personal*—it has to do with the baptismal reality that we are personally loved and accepted into son/daughter-ship with God through Christ. The second conversion into sharing the image of God through Christ *is social*—it has to do with discovering our vocational gifts in the community of the church, and then being sent out from the community through confirmation and reaffirmation. The third conversion *is cosmic*—it finally involves the sum total of our life's faith and work. It is our sharing with Christ in his death and in his resurrection. David Toolan, in his monumental work, <u>At Home in the Cosmos</u> explains our cosmic incorporation into Christ's Eucharistic dying and rising again:

> Jesus identifies with the earth…and consecrates the earth to new purposes. Of bread and wine, he says, "This is my body, take and eat…. This is my blood, take and drink."…Two great movements converge in what Jesus shows us here: the everlasting desire of cosmic dust to mean something great, and God's promise that it shall be done. There is first a centripetal movement [baptism and confirmation].[60] We the followers and disciples center in on Jesus, identify, become one with him. Then there is the centrifugal, decentralizing movement. Jesus, both conduit of Spirit-Energy and cosmic dust [God and human, citizen of heaven and earth], freely identifies himself with us and with the fruits of earth—the ash of the dying star present in bread and wine—and converts these gifts of earth, the work of human hands, into another story than the nightmarish one we have been telling with them….
>
> Jesus takes bread and wine…and metamorphoses them, transmutes them, breathes new meaning into them. In an allusion to the second chapter of the Book of Genesis, we are taken back to the original act of creation wherein "Yahweh God fashioned man of dust from the soil," and then "breathed into his nostrils a breath of life." Likewise, at the Last Supper Jesus breathes into inanimate earth-stuff (bread and wine) and converts them into signs of the eschatological "heavenly feast"….
>
> When Jesus says, "This is my body…This is my blood," and "Take and eat…Take and drink,"…He is bidding us to take in, to discover in our own soul-space the same Spirit that works in and through him. "So should the just soul be equal to God and close beside God," says Meister Eckhart (1260-1329), "not beneath or above."…
>
> Swallow this, Jesus effectively declares: I am God's promise for the elements, the exemplary inside of nature, its secret wish fulfilled.

Assume my role. Swallow my words, let them resonate in the marrow of your bones, and you will tap into the same current of Spirit that moves me. Swallow me and you will have taken in what God imagines for matter: that it is spirited, that justice be done to all, according to the great vision of the rainbow covenant We shall be one body, matter and spirit reconciled.

What is our function, our great work, in this vast cosmos?

When ancient eighth century Celts rose in the morning to pray, they prayed with a deep sense of connection to the material world: "I rise today through the strength of heaven: light of sun, radiance of moon, splendor of fire, speed of lighting, swiftness of wind, depth of sea, stability of earth, firmness of rock" (from St. Patrick's *Deer Cry*).... The universe's history, its groaning to give birth to something glorious, comes together in us.... We too, like Francis of Assisi are joined to nature at the hip.[61]

I am reminded here of Arthur Clarke's image in *2001: A Space Odyssey*, of mission commander Dave Bowman being reborn into a new humanity as he is shown floating in space as a gigantic fetus in a transparent womb. A reviewer of the epic film comments:

Bowman distinctly re-emerges within the embryo, with his own serene and wise-eyed features. He becomes a cosmic, innocent, orbiting "Star Child" that travels through the universe without technological assistance. The last enigmatic, open-ended image of the film is of the large, bright-eyed, glowing, luminous embryo in a translucent uterine amnion or bluish globe—an enhanced, reborn superhuman floating through space. Next to the globe of Earth on one-half of the screen is the Star Child's globe of about the same size. Its sphere dominates the screen in close-up before a final quick fade to black and following credits. The cyclical evolution from ape to man to spaceman to angel-starchild-superman is complete. Evolution has also been outwardly directed toward another level of existence—from isolated cave dwellings to the entire Earth to the Moon to the Solar System to the Universe. Humankind's unfathomed potential for the future is hopeful and optimistic, even though HAL (the computer) had momentarily threatened the evolution of humanity. What is the next stage in man's cosmic evolution beyond this powerful, immense, immortal, space-journeying creature?[62]

Clarke was interviewed on one of the major U.S., TV networks on the eve of the new millennium. He spoke hopefully of the future and recalled this image from *Space Odyssey*. Toolman continues:

> Offspring of stars, children of earth, we cannot be here simply to express our small personalities. Before the earth belonged to us, we belonged to the earth. We are here to take on duties to our fellow citizens of the earth, among which we must include plants, animals, and the soil…. We are *great-mothering* nature's soul-space, her heart and vocal chords—and her willingness, if we consent to do it, to be spirited, to be the vessel of the Holy One whose concern reaches out to embrace all that is created.[63]

In *Star Trek: The Motion Picture*, Captain Kirk and the crew of the star ship U.S.S. Enterprise, encounter a huge energy force with vast, never before known intelligence, who calls itself *"V'Ger,"* that is relentless in its pursuit to unite with its "Creator." Near the end of the story, a human female image of *V'Ger* (who resembles Ilia, a missing officer from the Enterprise) merges with Will Decker, one of Kirk's officers and there is a magnificent theophany of light and color as a new evolutionary life form is given birth. The union takes place because the "creature, *"V'Ger* is lonely for her Creator, and she will not rest until communion is reached—a time when she downloads (communicates) all of her gathered data (her-story). It turns out that *V.G.E.R.* is a NASA space probe (Voyager VI) sent out to gather all of the universe's knowledge and then return to its source to report its findings.

Captured imaginatively in this story is a reflection of the same Eucharistic drama that seeks to take the story of Christ and give permission to creation to embody that story by integrating all of creation's components into a meaningful oneness. The Christian task is to reconcile the divisions of the cosmos, and then to sing the song of its new glory. The Creator has given the privilege of that task to humankind by incarnating God's Logos into creation as a means to empower and grace this cosmic vocation.

When our sabbatical pilgrimage brought us to London, we witnessed a lively and sizable gathering of "Treky pilgrims" going to a two-month long exhibition of Star Trek history, paraphernalia, and personalities. Star Trek is a kind of contemporary epic pilgrimage that tries to give meaning and hope to our present time. We, who have seen another Great Star, need to recapture the imagination of the "trekies" of our time and invite them to share with us in writing the story of God's cosmic vocation, and in living it out. Tooman speaks to the trekies of our day as he speaks of the "big theo-logical drama:"

We are nature's black box, her vessel of soul-space—and hence her last chance to become spirited, to be the vessel of God, the carrier of the message that all creation is not only "very good," but to be glorified. That's the script, the big theo-logical drama. We are the voice of nature, "the voice of the hurricane, this thermal howl."…Do you not hear the entire creation groaning, aspiring in one great act of giving birth? And do you not hear the appeal…that earth makes of us?…Do you not hear the stars, the algae, the forests and mitochondria calling out to you—to name them properly, to understand them, to give them voice, to give them meaning by what we make of this earth?[64]

Just as our sabbatical time began, Tolkien's *The Two Towers*, the second part of the epic *Lord of the Rings* trilogy, opened in movies theatres across the western world. Tolkien, like C. S. Lewis (who was a personal friend), had a near death experience in serving his country at a time of war. It has been speculated that in these experiences of fighting, and almost dying, against an impersonal presence of evil, Tolkien and Lewis felt themselves trapped in a metallic and mechanical drama where they were powerless, and in which they could discern no real meaning. Consequently, their therapy was to write imaginative epic journeys that finally give meaning to life in the midst of our humanity's battle with the horrendous and meaningless expressions of personified Evil. In the movie version of Tolkien's *Two Towers,* there is a battle scene where the good forces of the earth fight against the twin towers (which are symbols in the story of personified evil). All of creation's forces unite as they never have before to fight a great cosmic battle. My favorite scene is where the great old trees of the dark forest come alive, with voice and legs, to join in creation's great battle. A victorious and meaningful future for creation is only possible when all of its constituent and variant species (hobits, elves, dwarfs, fairies, humans, trees, etc) unite into an ecological team effort. Tooman continues:

> Isn't that what we are here for: the secret mission of the scientist's inquiries, the homemaker's labor, the builder's dream? To pour soul into the soul-less, into the chaos of nature, and make all creation "shudder with joy," as the Creator-Poet did on the first day?…We are placed in a radically unfinished universe, where it is our task to bring things to completion.[65]

Tooman, Tolkien, Lewis, Clarke, the creators of Star Trek and countless others today trying to visualize a viable and just future, are not just writers of science fiction. They are a responsible part of God's cosmic Logos struggling to discern a life worth dying for—a life that will finally fulfill the urge in all of us to unite with our creator.

So, we are called to join with the incarnate Logos, to not only redeem the cosmos, but with Christ, to be raised in and with it. The Christ journey story always finishes with transformation and resurrection. It is not just a story about death and reconciling past enmities; it is also a story about birthing new life and re-creation. It is a four-fold Eucharistic drama calling us to:

(1) Incarnate in and with all the mighty wonders of creation,

(2) Listen to the voices of creation and its Creator, and receive its Blessings of empowerment,

(3) Struggle with and die to the old ways that have separated us from each other and consciousness from unconsciousness, and finally

(4) Integrate our separate stories of resurrection into Christ's One Story of Heaven, and sing it out—share it with the Triune Source of Glory.

Exercises:

1. Recall (or journal) a story about your coming to grips with your baptismal identity.

2. Recall (or journal) a story about your coming to grips with your vocational call.

3. Spend some time journaling about your "place of resurrection" and your "retirement." Connect this reflection with what you would like your tombstone to say about you and the meaning of your life.

4. Reflect on (or journal) the great struggles you have fought (are fighting) in your life. Where do you see a connection between your battles of death and resurrection, and those of Jesus?

5. If you haven't already done so, plan your funeral: its place, lessons, music, mood, participants, your place of internment, etc. Share your plan with your family. Give it to your priest for safe keeping.

Section Seven

Developing Habits of the Heart for Living in the Presence of God

Reflections on Life's Road

Some people travel in straight lines:
Sit in metal boxes, eyes ahead,
Always mindful of their target,
Moving in obedience to colored lights and white lines,
Mission accomplished at journey's end.

Some people travel round in circles:
Trudging in drudgery, eyes looking down,
Knowing only too well their daily, unchanging round,
Moving in response to clock and habit,
Journey never finished yet never begun.

I want to travel in patterns of God's making:
Walking in wonder, gazing all around,
Knowing my destiny, though not my destination,
Moving to the rhythm of the surging of the spirit,
A journey which when life ends, in Christ has just begun.[66]
—Julie McGuinness

Christian pilgrims have traditionally sought guides and road maps for their journeys. "How to" and "Do it yourself" guidebooks tend to be best sellers in today's book stores. Yet, in my experience, the idea of *discipline* tends to scare off many would-be journeyers into the interior life. Perhaps, Julie McGuiness is right in wanting to find a way forward that is not described in regimented straight lines, nor in fruitless circles, but a way that might be described as fitting the design of our own particular soul, uniquely created by the Creator's imagination—a way forward that allows us to playfully co-create in the freedom of our imaginations, while at the same time being coached by practices that are known to work for fellow journeyers whose soul terrains are similar to our own.

Ian Bradley asks a provocative question in his monumental work, *Colonies of Heaven: Celtic Models for Today's Church*:

> Could it be that in the post-modern, pick—and-mix spiritual supermarket we now inhabit, people are actually craving commitment, discipline and obedience?[67]

In my seminary days and in the ten years or so that followed, I tried very hard to work out a rule of life (spiritual disciplines) that were taught by the great monastic traditions, i.e., Benedictine, Ignatian, Franciscan, Dominican, etc.; or by the many manuals for spiritual practices that were available in those days. I cannot begin to number the days I fell asleep at my prayer desk trying to fit my soul into the right rhythm of meditation and spiritual discipline. Nothing quite fit. Was I a misfit, a hopeless would-be athlete for God incapable of finding a stride that would enable me to go the long distance?

What a relief it was to read of the work of Carl Jung, and the many authors in the 70's—90's who applied Jung's personality typing to the life of the soul. I finally began to find those habits of the soul that fit my peculiar soul-shape. I confess that I am still experimenting and changing my diet of spiritual disciplines. Changing outward demands and changing times, as well as some growth in my own maturity, have challenged me to continue to experiment under the tutelage of a spiritual director who keeps me honest and accountable.

In the Desert and Wells workshops that I have led over the years, I have found that asking "like-souled" participants to group together and work out their own ways forward, has been fruitful and much appreciated. In the end each of us needs to accept responsibility for this task, for only we know the tendencies and secrets of our own desert's darkness, and its corresponding needs for illumination and nourishment.

A number of years ago I suggested to the clergy of the diocese of Eastern Michigan that they experiment with transforming their Confirmation classes and

Adult Inquirers classes into what we were then calling "Discovery Classes." The idea behind this was that instead of just introducing new disciples to the history, traditions and etiquette of our Episcopal denomination, why not also emphasize the spiritual disciplines that the new confirmands would be able to use in their ongoing journey as God's new apostles. The five proposed disciplines were:

(1) Read Mark's Gospel and describe how your own life's journey could be transformed to reflect the way Jesus lived his life.
(2) Take on and report to your class a ministry project that will utilize your own special giftedness in responding to some person's or some group's particular needs.
(3) Make an annual financial commitment to your church and/or to some altruistic community agency.
(4) Introduce a friend to the Christian faith by bringing them to church and by sharing your journey of faith with them.
(5) Formulate a rule of life and share it with the class.

These five proposed requisites for joining the church give hints to what forming a new spiritual path forward into a deeper spirituality could consist of. Spiritual disciplines that might be part of a new rule of life or personal mission statement could include any of the following (and perhaps others of your own imagining). The point is they need to fit your own particular giftedness as well as your own particular vulnerabilities. The following list is long and is not meant to overwhelm. It is best to choose a few practices, rather than to take on too many and not follow through on your good intentions.

Bible reading; church and community service; acts of stewardship; acts of evangelism; reading prayers out loud; meditation (prayer of the imagination); contemplation (prayer of silence and solitude); prayers of intercession; prayers of adoration, praise and thanksgiving; prayers of contrition and confession; reading the daily office from the Book of Common Prayer, or some other prayer book; reading the lives of Christian heroes and heroines; reading books of Christian spirituality and of theology; spend regular time with a spiritual director or a soul friend; diet; fast; regularly examine your conscience—using the Orthodox Eight Sins; or the Ten Commandments or the Beatitudes as guideposts; attend public worship (especially Eucharistic worship) with regularity; join and spend committed time with a cell group, prayer group or bible study group; journal daily, or as frequently as you are able, about how God is present and not present in your life; engage in regular physical exercise; get regular rest; go on a personal or on a group spiritual pilgrimages; write poetry or prose about your experiences of God and life; share in a Christian teaching ministry, or in another teaching ministry that helps others to grow; spend regular time in solitude ("stop, look and listen" for God[68]); receive the sacrament of unction and laying on of hands (healing) when you are ill; sing or listen to music; walk; visit water ways or mountains and seek out God's presence there; go on a guided retreat; participate in a class of spiritual instruction; paint, draw, or sculpture; experience theatre and drama; listening to and journaling about your dreams; engage in playful activity; laugh with others; imagine yourself in God's presence; pray the Jesus Prayer over and over again ("Jesus, my Lord and Savior"), or pray some other prayer mantra; etc.

While there are many ingredients to a rule or way of life that could fit your particular personality and soul-shape, there are distinct spiritual practices that are almost universally helpful in nurturing our continuing spiritual formation. I would put these following elements as a beginning frame for a rule for you to experiment with:

I. **Disciplines to nurture a *Communal* spirituality** that continue your baptismal conversion towards your true *identity*:

    a. A committed membership in a Christian Church or fellowship, including regular participation in a Sunday Eucharist.

    b. A committed membership in a small group that meets at least monthly (preferably bi-weekly or weekly) and practices regular prayer, study, personal accountability and mutual spiritual support.

II. **Disciplines to nurture a *Conversational* spirituality** that continue your chrismatic (confirmation and reaffirmation) conversion towards your true *vocation*:

    a. Daily (the goal, though not always attainable) time of entering into the presence of God where you "stop, look and listen" for God. This time would normally include period times of bible reading, intercession, confession, thanksgiving and adoration.

    b. Regular time (at least four times a year; monthly times might become a goal) with a spiritual director or soul friend. I will say more about this later.

III. **Disciplines to nurture a *Compassionate* spirituality** that continue your Eucharistic conversion towards your true *ultimate purpose* or "*martyrdom.*"

    a. Regular commitment to the ministry of presence and hospitality to needy or pre-Christian people.

    b. Regular commitment to the ministry of reconciliation in confronting the evils of injustice.

Soul Friendship

A person without a soul friend is like a body without a head.

—Brigid of Kildare

I can only truly know myself through the other.

—Jean-Paul Sartre

Of all the gifts that a Wise Providence grants us to make a life full and happy, friendship is the most beautiful.

—Epicurius

Before moving on to the next section, I want to highlight a particularly important discipline for a vigorous spiritual life. For Celtic Christians, having a soul friend, was the most important characteristic and most essential requirement for maintaining a healthy spiritual life.

When we visited Ray Simpson on the Holy Island of Lindisfarne, he shared with us that he found that he had to write a book about soul friendship (*Soul Friendship: Celtic Insights into Spiritual Mentoring*, 1999) as it was becoming a subject about which he was being overwhelmingly asked to talk about. In his book Simpson suggests that…

> Our lives need reference points. We need people to whom we can pour out our immediate problems, yes, but also to whom we can explore the meaning of our soul's anguish and aspirations…. The benefits of Christian soul befriending relate to much more than a person's career. They relate to the whole person—body, mind and spirit. They relate to both practical matters of the present and to a person's eternal destiny. Only if we know ourselves and be known by another can we grow into the likeness of God, which is our destiny.
>
> Although there is some overlap between soul friendship and mentoring or counseling, there is a vital difference. We mostly use a mentor to develop aptitudes and attitudes that will improve our performance or advance our career. We mostly use a therapist or a counselor to help solve a problem, or to function better within our existing values. We use a tutor mostly to increase our knowledge. These helpers are used for a part of our life. A soul friend, however, is used for the whole of life.
>
> The soul friend may use some of the tools of the counselor or of the mentor, but for a different purpose. In soul befriending your main aim

is not to solve problems (though you may need to do that 'on the way'); your aim is to achieve wholeness. Often counselors are trained not to let a client get to them, whereas a soul friend might, on appropriate occasions, share something of their own vulnerabilities in order to encourage a seeker to unlock theirs. The model of wholeness that a Christian soul friend uses is Jesus Christ, not the latest theory of this or that psychologist.

The purpose of the soul friend is to help the seeker discover where they are, and what should be their next steps in their journey through life, in the light of eternity. A third person is always invited to be a full partner; that third person is the Holy Spirit of God.[69]

A Note to the Clergy about Spiritual Direction

How important is it that clergy have spiritual direction? How important is it for their ability to pastor effectively; as well as for their own personal wellness, and for their family's wellness? Margaret Guenther, who before her recent retirement was Professor of Ascetical Theology at General Seminary, answered that question in a recent interview:

> Spiritual direction for clergy is terribly important…. I know for myself I need to see my director just to stay honest. I think we are really in danger of spiritual arrogance if we think such things as, "I am God's right hand and I can do this." Or "I'm too advanced spiritually to go and have someone else listen to me." So spiritual direction is vital to clergy wellness in that it keeps us healthy and honest and reminds us of who we are. It is a great idea to have every clergy person to have some person in their lives who does this. It might be a cleric, a lay person, a person from a religious order…. As clergy, we need to cultivate…openness and perhaps get over our own inhibitions in talking about prayer. Sometimes it much easier to lead prayer in public than sit down with another person and say, "Let's talk about prayer."…spiritual direction is under-utilized…. Even if, as clergy, we don't do or offer traditional spiritual direction, we have those conversations and relationships that partake of the quality of spiritual direction. As clergy, if we are with someone who is facing death, someone who is living with a debilitating illness, someone who is living with a great concern of addiction in the family, or who is living with concern for children, we will have those conversations—not where we are fixing the person or offering solutions—but where we are trying to sit with them as another Christian and say, "Where is God in all of this?" We probably won't have an answer, but even if don't name it—if we're good pastors—we're going to find ourselves doing ad hoc spiritual direction…. In the future, the importance of spiritual direction will increase for clergy. We have to acknowledge this thirst of people to understand who they are in the sight of God…. Spiritual direction is the good part of ministry. It is the cream. It is the dessert.[70]

Let me reiterate: Anyone who gives spiritual direction, whether formally or informally, ought also to be receiving it.

Exercises:

1. Draft an experimental rule of life, and share it with a trusted friend. Try it out for at least a month and then review and revamp it to fit the realities of your life and needs of your soul.

2. Draw up a list of people you are acquainted with to whom you are naturally drawn. Cross out those with whom you could not sustain thoughtful, rounded conversations about things of the mind. Now cross out those with whom you could not sustain a sharing of the deep things of the spirit, because intimacies would either not be understood or not be respected. If anyone remains on this list, what prevents you taking further steps to develop the friendship?[71]

3. Carefully go through the Eight Sins or Vices listed in section five of this Guide. Discern which of these vices your soul-type is most vulnerable to. Then prayerfully dream up a means by which you can confront and remedy each of these vices. Keep a journal of your spiritual warfare and rejoice in your victories.

4. If you are interesting in exploring more deeply the value of having a spiritual director, read Eugene Peterson's exploration of what a spiritual director is and does in <u>Under the Unpredictable Plant</u> (Eerdmans, 1992), pp. 182-190.

5. Practice the Celtic "Caim."[72]
    Visualize yourself encircled by the love, the light, the peace of God. Make a circle by using the index finger of your right hand, extending your arm and slowly turning clockwise until you make a circle in which you are enclosed. Then say:

    > Circle me, O God, keep peace within trouble without
    > Circle me, O God, keep love within hatred without
    > Circle me, O God, keep light within and darkness out.

    Learn to rest in that love, that light, that peace. Know that God is with you, before you and behind you. God will protect you from your past and in the future. Let God's presence give you light, love, and peace. Then, radiate the love and light and peace. Visualize other people surrounded by God and immersed in God's presence. Envision the people you pray for; see them surrounded by God's light, love and peace—know that this is a real.

Section Eight

Visioning a "Village of Heaven" for Today's Future Church

*It may well be highly desirable for churches to build core groups of members who act as a kind of **monasterium**, perhaps sharing a common rule of life and disciplines of prayer. We should not forget, however, the variety of ministries found within the Celtic monastery which sprang from a recognition of different levels and expressions of commitment to Christ, as well as of different gifts and callings. The **monasteria** were essentially open communities, providing staging posts for seekers as well as homes to the committed. We should have this dual role and this sense of variety and balance in mind **as we seek to plant our colonies of heaven today.**[73]*

—Ian Bradley

During these past seven years as I have immersed myself and the diocese in the cultures of congregational development and renewal, I have observed that the evolving processes and rationales for "church planting" has been promoted as one of the most promising hopes for future church growth and church renewal. I too harbor such a hope, and look forward to the day when the Diocese of Eastern Michigan bravely launches its first new church plant. However, deep in my soul, I know that the real challenge for rebuilding tomorrow's church has to do with the spirit; and not just with strategically placed geographic centers for new buildings or new gathered communities with or without their own buildings. At the heart and soul of the matter, is the reawakening of the spirit—it's a matter of rekindling a passionate (Celtic like) spirituality.

There is a place where much of the new strategy for church planting coincides with the challenge to awaken a passionate spirituality; and that point of intersection has to do with building and encouraging a new way of coming together *in community* as the People of God. Let's honestly face the fact that much of what passes for congregational community today (i.e., Sunday services, and for a few, weekday church life) lacks the ability to fully nurture the kind of spirituality that we have been talking about in the previous seven sections of this Guide.

As helpful as gathering for Eucharist and hearing a good sermon are, these spiritual enrichments are just not enough for many of today's hungry and thirsty seekers, who are yearning for a "hearth" all week long that will warm and guide them on a more regular basis then once, or even four times a month for an hour. Recent church research suggests that those churches that are growing, or more importantly, those that are spiritually "healthy" are those who have cell or house groups that meet regularly in addition to their Sunday gathering for corporate worship. These sub-communities keep their size small enough so that deep and lasting intimacy, trust and accountability can be achieved. In some ways these sub-communities or small "villages of heaven" as I like to call them, give back to contemporary Western society what we had in small village communities before the industrial and technological revolutions transformed and fragmented our family and church communities which served as our bases for spiritual nurturing.

Reforming congregational structures is not the only need the church has today as it seeks to awaken a passionate spirituality. There is also the need for diocesan, provincial and national church structures to reform. Ian Bradley suggests that the single most important thing that the contemporary church can glean from Celtic (monastic) Christianity is to somehow recapture their genius for adaptability and vulnerability expressed in their practice of "pilgrimage." Bradley gives us this counsel:

> A pilgrim church lives lightly to buildings, financial support, and hierarchies. Too many churches today, feeling beleaguered and threatened,

have abandoned pilgrimage and provisionality for an outlook and structure more appropriate to narrow sectarianism. There is much wisdom in
Jean Vanier's observation that "a sect has control at its heart, a community
has journey at its heart."[74]

In a more radical reflection, Bradley gets more controversial and "personal" as
he urges us to:

> ...be prepared to let churches die. Too many are at present kept
> going with the equivalent of artificial life-support systems that should
> be switched off. Churches which can serve as hubs of modern monastic
> families should be built up and supported. Radiating from them, like
> spokes of a wheel, would be cells, house churches and other groups
> probably operated out of a more provisional and temporary prem-
> ise...New churches and old, charismatic and traditional, liberal and
> conservative, would be held together by the provision of a broad-based
> ministry team reflecting different theological and liturgical styles,
> working from a central resource base and sharing a communal perspec-
> tive while operating in a variety of different styles and locations.[75]

This could well be the kind of church that our grandchildren will experience.
God and time will tell. In the meanwhile, what can we (as a still new and some-
what flexible diocese) do to become more of a community emphasizing *journey*,
than a sect emphasizing *control*? This is not a new question for our diocese.
Perhaps the idea that was talked about as the diocese was forming not too many
years ago of a bishop traveling in a mobile house trailer spending most of her/his
time out in the field, has some merit after all. What is missing, in that vision of
provisionality and vulnerability, is an image and methodology for re-forming and
building "hearth" communities that will form, nurture, sustain, and send out
tomorrow's spiritually mature Christians. What is also missing in that earlier
vision is an understanding that renewal must have a collegial leadership base, not
just the charismatic or pastoral or teaching leadership of one bishop.

There is another phenomenon to look at for what God is currently doing in
the church to rebuild it into new "hearth" villages of spiritual health. I am referring to the rapid proliferation of ecumenical (with significant Anglican con-
stituencies) Celtic and Benedictine like communities that are geographically
spread out, but who share a common life through following a common worship
style, and a common rule of life. These communities usually have two kinds of
membership: one that is highly committed and centrally housed in a kind of
monastic family configuration; and one that is geographically spread out with its

own cell bases that are accountable to the central structure through an annual conference and seasonal leadership retreats. Examples of such communities would be the *Taize Community* based at Taize, France; the *Northumbria Community* of northeastern England; the *Iona Community* based on the Isle of Iona in Scotland; the *Community of Aidan and Hilda,* based on The Holy Island of Lindisfarne in Northumbria, England; and the *Order of Julian of Norwich*, based in Waukesha, Wisconsin. England, Wales, Scotland and the United States seem to have the correct "fertile soil" to draw, encourage, and sustain these new experiments that may well shape tomorrow's church. I would list here the *House of Prayer* in Collegeville, Minnesota. While there is not a resident monastic family here, the House of Prayer does have a regular rhythm of worship, and does seek to be a leaven of spiritual nurture, geographically situated right in the middle of the Episcopal Diocese of Minnesota.

Bradley refers to these communities in the following manner:

> How do we begin to keep in time with the deep pulsations of Eternity and establish colonies of heaven in a society that is profoundly earthborn, materialistic and secular? One way is by establishing communities which embrace many of the disciplines of monasticism and have a resident group at their core, but which attract substantial numbers of adherents who do not practice communal living.[76]

My spirit is lifted up as I rehearse in my memory the many signs of revitalized community in our diocese:

- The Vision conferences
- The Alpha courses
- The many new cell groups that have begun to form
- The desire to become a proactive (apostolic) community
- The desire to a people of "miraculous expectation"
- The desire for "grassroots mission"
- The Breaking New Ground: Transforming Lives initiative
- The Call Waiting Conference
- A willingness to continue to experiment and restructure
- A willingness to participate in leadership and congregational development
- A pervading thirst for God's Spirit

God is present and active among us. Let us thank God for that. But there is now a need for us to focus on our being—on our spiritual life.

At this point I would dare to propose a draft (for grass roots conversation) for what might be necessary in forming regional "hearth" villages for awakening passionate spirituality. I shall be using the terms "hearth group," "village of heaven," and "cell or house group" interchangeably. They are all nurturing sub-communities that seek to awaken and sustain a passionate spirituality. I believe such communities are most effective when they embody the following (distinctively Celtic) characteristics:

1. **A common worship format for daily prayer.** Prayer must always be at the root of building healthy Christian community. During my sabbatical time I have been experimenting with enriching my morning office prayer time. I have borrowed from three relatively new Celtic based prayer books: The Celtic Book of Offices (produced by the Northumbria Community), The Glenstal Book of Prayer (produced by the monks of Glenstal Abbey, a Benedictine community located in Murroe, County Limerick, Ireland), and A Holy Island Prayer Book (written by Ray Simpson for the Order of Aidan and Hilda). Finding a morning office prayer style that fit my soul-shape has been an enriching experience. Over time, a hearth community can reshape its common prayer into a shape that fits its particular community's soul-shape.

2. **A common rule of life (spiritual disciplines).** This can be simple or complex depending on the spiritual needs and aspirations of the community. The rule for the Northumbrian Community is summarized in two words: "adaptability & vulnerability." The rule for Taize has five components: (1) Daily bible reading and intercessory prayer from a common lectionary, (2) ten percent tithe, (3) a balanced use of time for work, leisure, family, skill development, worship and devotions, and for rest and sleep, (4) action for justice and peace, and (5) participation in a local cell group and in larger plenary gatherings. The research and prayer that I have done on this sabbatical has led me to propose a "life-journeying" rule (section seven, page 83) based on the "three conversions" to Christ in the context of our self identity in community, our social vocation through the church, and our final commitment to the earth.

3. **A resident team of excellence.** Celtic monastic communities helped to "save western civilization" during the dark ages because they were centers of ministerial excellence. Pastoral care; soul-friend mentoring; liturgical forms; libraries and scriptoriums of biblical, spiritual and cultural literature; architectural and

artistic design; poetry and story telling; agriculture and animal husbandry; house keeping: all of these ministries were represented by various monks, nuns, and laity in the community. In our visits to some of the more lively cathedrals of England and Wales these past few months, I have observed a growing interest in growing ministry teams with multi-disciplinary specialties. Canterbury and Norwich Cathedrals (and others) are re-visioning themselves as regional centers for spiritual and ministry formation. A more modest "hearth" community for generating passionate spirituality might have a minimum of three specialists: one for worship, one for teaching, and one for pastoral care. A resident artist or poet would be a marvelous bonus.

4. **A center for hospitality**. When Ira and I entered the arched gate of the ancient monastic site at Glendalough, Marcus Losack, our guide said that we had entered a place of sacred sanctuary where we were safe from the world's darkness, and where God's grace was liberally shared with all who entered. The ancient monastic communities of men and woman, single and married were places that received any and all who wished sanctuary. You didn't even have to be a Christian. All that was required was your desire to be in this special God-place, where you were free to discover who you were in amidst a community of God's caring disciples. How could this be emulated today? If there is a shared residence, an extra bedroom would fulfill this Celtic and Benedictine characteristic. If there is not a shared residence, then the spirit of hospitality could be realized by individual families who had extra house space and who had the gift of hospitality. Today we are becoming all too aware that Christians are not formed by simply being involved in hour long rituals of Baptism, Confirmation, and Holy Communion. These sacramental rites of passage are there to mark and celebrate the life-long passages to Christian maturity. Seekers need places of refuge (whether in the local congregation or in monastic like "hearth" communities of hospitality) not to be told what to believe, but to discover in loving community and in loving conversation who they are and what it is God wants them to do with their lives.

5. **A common table for sharing food and fellowship**. A home (or a community) cannot be a home (or community) without a table. Many languages connect the root meanings of bread with family or community. Jesus instituted the Last Supper, understanding full well the connection that the common meal had to building the community of his Body. While the Sunday observance of the Eucharist already serves to nurture our need to unite us to our life in Christ, the more localized agape meal or simple meal, shared in a cell group or a "hearth" sub-community, builds spiritual intimacy with those who are

your closest and most trusted spiritual allies. Most sub-communities of compassionate spirituality that I have experienced or heard about have built in times of table fellowship.

6. **Awareness for the need for sabbatical-time and pilgrimage-space.** As I previously mentioned, the practice of pilgrimage was an outstanding characteristic of Celtic Christianity. I did not know how important these past three months of sabbatical-time and pilgrimage—space would be to my spiritual well being until I actually ventured out and did what I knew God wanted me to do. My sense of personal identity, my sense of vocational call, and my growing acceptance about my place of resurrection could not have been realized to the degree that have been without this sabbatical time. I suspect that my time away from the diocese has also been good for the diocese: giving other diocesan leaders an opportunity to share in episcopal-like functions; as well as giving the diocese a breather, a time away from my catalytic and sometimes over-energetic leadership style. I am told that Eugene Peterson (author of many excellent and perceptive books on the spiritual life and translator of the popular <u>Message</u> version of the Old and New Testaments) took a three month sabbatical *every year* of his time in congregational ministry. He claims that his sabbatical time was the primary reason that his pastorate was so effective, and that his ministry was filled with such joy. The sabbatical is the best tool that I know of to fight the battle against the tyranny and illusion of western materialism, consumerism, and spiritual emptiness. If you want your priest to be healthier, happier and more effective send her/him on a sabbatical. Of course the value of the sabbatical applies across the board to all people, including house-wives/husbands, single people and the unemployed. The challenge is to build in an economic where-with-all for the sabbatical to occur. Sabbatical/pilgrimage awareness may be the least practiced characteristic of sub-communities for passionate spirituality. I pray this will change.

A Celtic Image for the Future?

The Diocese of Eastern Michigan does not have a cathedral. I believe about one in ten of our U.S. Episcopal dioceses are without cathedrals. Cathedrals have been historically helpful and unhelpful. They have been beneficial to the diocese when they served in a servant capacity as a place to model and teach what was most Christ-like and most effective for congregational ministry. Cathedrals have ill served the church when they have become political empires of self-serving power, and show places of prestigious ambition. It is good to see the current movement within Anglicanism where the Cathedral is reshaping its servant role towards serving the diocese as a place of spiritual and skill formation.

Before Henry VIII destroyed all of the English abbeys, in a sixteenth century power move, the abbeys, in their best days, were hearths of spiritual formation and islands of prayer. They were places where peasants as well as sons and daughters of kings could come to learn and to dedicate their lives to God in prayer and simple service—all to the benefit of the people. In Celtic Ireland, before the twelfth century Norman invasions, it was the abbeys of the monastic cities that served the people. Void of the Latin and Saxon geographic parish structure, there was little need for cathedrals or bishops or for parish congregations. Abbots and abbesses with their armies of ordained and lay monks and nuns were the pastoral and teaching ministers of their day. There is much in common today with the "hearth" sub-communities of passionate (Celtic like) spirituality and the abbey-monastic structures of Celtic Ireland, Wales, Scotland and England.

What would it be like if Eastern Michigan was to birth, from its grassroots polity and structure, a comparable community or communities? What would a diocesan community of hearth groups and villages look like with an "abbot-based," spiritually healthy leadership? I am not sure that I know what this would look like in practice. It may be an impractical pie-in-the-sky idea. And yet when I mentioned this, in passing, to Ray Simpson, who is the respected and distinguished Guardian of the Community of Aidan and Hilda at Lindisfarne, his eyes immediately lit up, and he felt compelled to tell me not to think of this as wild and impossible dream. What do you think?

Exercises:

1.   What is God doing in your congregation? Where is God "visible" in your congregation? Is God trying to lead your congregation in a particular direction? What are you doing to support God's movement in your congregation? What might you do that you are not presently doing?

2.   How does your congregation and its sub-communities nurture and feed your spiritual needs? Are there spiritual needs that you have, that are not being met? If so, what are they? Consider sharing your thoughts about this with another member of your congregation and with your clergy.

3.   List all of the nurturing Christian sub-communities that exist in your congregation, convocation, and local community. Do you belong to any of them? If not, which one of these might be helpful to nurturing your spiritual growth? If you do belong to some form of "hearth" group, which of the six mentioned characteristics in this section are present in your group? Which are absent? Would there be some value in introducing any of the missing (assuming there are some) characteristics into your group?

Section Nine

Conclusion:
Awakening to Begin Again

"When God created us, God gave Adam a secret—and that secret was not how to begin, but how to begin again. In other words, it is not given to us to begin, that privilege is God's alone. But it is given to us to begin again—and we do every time we choose to defy death and side with the living."77

—Elie Wiesel

"When I heard that my friend, Bishop Ken Untener (bishop of the Diocese of Saginaw) had died on March 27, my Good Friday began a week early. Why did someone who was so real, so fruitful, so transparent and Grace filled have to die? Why did Jesus have to die?

*Then Palm Sunday's lesson from the Epistle to the Philippians reminded me that Jesus **chose** to die, "to be obedient to the point of death—even on a cross" giving us "an example of his great humility."*

I know well that Bishop Ken, like Jesus, embraced his death in his baptismal promise to become, as he said, "our waiter." Bishop Ken long ago decided to die his death every day with a purpose. He "couldn't save his life, but he could save the lives of many others." When he repeatedly made space for those he knew; when he sold his mansion to become available to any who asked for time; when he rolled up his sleeves, dressed like the rest of us, encouraging us to live our lives to the fullest—he demonstrated that "letting go and letting God" was the Way of life.

Easter is in all of this. Perhaps Easter is really about being given permission to freely give our lives away for others. We need no longer fear death once we have given our lives to God. We have been given life simply to give it away. Whenever we do that, "Spring" comes into God's creation.

Thank you Bishop Ken, for exemplifying the Paschal mystery—the mystery of Easter that shouts out that darkness and death have been, are now, and will be overcome by the death and Resurrection of Jesus. Alleluia, once again this mystery has been reflected in the lives of one of His saints."

—Ed Leidel, *The Saginaw News*, Easter 2004

I am writing this summary section the week after my friend and bishop of the Roman Catholic Diocese of Saginaw died unexpectedly of leukemia. Bishop Ken Untener served his diocese faithfully for twenty five years and became a living icon of servant ministry. Bishop Untener's first words to his diocese after consecration were, "I am going to be your waiter." He quickly maneuvered to sell the bishop's "palace," and then began to live out of the back of his car moving temporarily into parish parsonages throughout the diocese. His infectious ability to build community and networks gave him the aura of becoming a kind of traveling "hearth" for drawing people of all faiths to God's warming presence of promise and possibility. Bishop Ken modeled a new kind of ecclesial leadership. Ken was an itinerant abbot bishop.

Bishop Ken demonstrated that it is possible in the midst of institutional weariness to awaken spiritual sensitivities and begin again. Uncounted thousands of the grassroots of Mid-Michigan grieved and celebrated Bishop Ken's amazing life as his funeral liturgy was aired on two mid-Michigan television stations. Ken had a grassroots spirituality that was manifest in the life that he led.

There is a spiritual hearth at the heart of every person, congregation and diocese. There is something of a Ken Untener in each of us. This Guide has attempted to give a blueprint for rekindling hearth fires. The fire is ignitable precisely where we have a passion to begin again in the face of immense community and cultural brokenness. Perhaps there has never been a time in history where the need for rekindling has matched so strongly with the individual and communal desire to "begin again."

With drama, alarm and promise Rick Joyner defines our times in an unpublished booklet for Celtic style house churches and cell groups seeking to find a new way of being church.

"We are now entering one of the greatest watershed periods in human history. Creation itself is charged with the electricity of these times and is beginning to groan and travail for what is about to come…. In preparation for this greatest of events the church is about to go through a metamorphosis. She is going to change from a worm to a butterfly. A caterpillar is confined to the earth, and its path must conform to the contour of the earth. Likewise, for nearly two thousand years the church has often conformed more to the ways of the world than to the ways of the Spirit. Soon the church will go through a change so dramatic that she will seem to emerge as an entirely different creature. It will be like another birth…."[78]

This guide was intended to be used as a tool to ready and nurture souls who want to claim a new way of being church for tomorrow. The vision described here has been Celtic in origin. The tools have been refreshments of ancient Celtic ways:

- Embracing tears for rekindling new beginnings (section one)
- Searching for and building spiritual communities of support (section two)
- Examining and reintegrating our lifestyles for balance (section three)
- Discovering and naming our gateways to God's Presence (section four)
- Learning to dance around our own "well of Grace" in the midst of our particular desert (section five)
- Naming and sharing the great conversion stories of our spiritual journeys (section six)
- Developing new habits for hearts to sustain our spiritual quests (section seven)
- Re-visioning diocesan or regional "villages of heaven" to connect and nurture our personal and congregational hearth places of the heart. (section eight)

God's Energy in Life Cycles

Life has been created to live in rhythms that coincide with God's journeying presence with us. The rhythms of the changing seasons and the rhythm of day and night connected to the sun and the rotation of our earth on a skewed axis; the rhythms of the tides and of insect and bird migration patterns connected to the moon's orbit around our earth; the mysterious rhythms of birth cycles; the rhythm of the birth and death of stars—these and countless other cycles within our universe reflect the urge and promise of birth, death, and rebirth. The Celts taught that life is a great circle with all of us joining with our Creator at the end.

Most important to us is the given rhythm of our humanity revealed to us in the birth, life, crucifixion and resurrection of Jesus of Nazareth. As we engage the seasons of the Church year in our worship, we connect Jesus life cycle with our own life journey and continue to become icons of His resurrected life for others.

Arlin Routhage[79] has suggested that faith communities like people also go through life cycles.

"The Church year and the faith journey are lived out in the same way. Birth is celebrated in Advent and Christmas. Formation in life and growing up is observed in the season of Epiphany. The stability of life when goals are accomplished is lived in Pentecost. The decline of life is experienced in the season of Lent. Then, the cycle begins all over again in rebirth at Easter. Rothauge assets that the same life cycle is lived in parish churches. Congregational development is enabling them to experience new birth by beginning new life before a decline begins in the period of stability. He calls the beginning on new things while the old continues 'parallel development.' This is the 'two tiered' model of the Celtic Christians in ministry."[80]

The time for parallel development or "new beginnings" is most pregnant at the end of Pentecost, just as Advent begins—a time where there is still energy to listen and re-engage. This is the time to be aware of unique appearances in our lives— the time of becoming aware of God's movement suddenly present in miraculous expectations. Our diocese was richly blessed in 2003 and in 2004 by teaching visits from Rob Voyle,[81] a psychologist and Anglican priest who applies the work of "Appreciative Inquiry" to discerning God's ever present mission in the midst of our lives. The process of appreciative inquiry assumes that God's project of blessing, healing, reconciliation, and resurrected new Life is already present and active in our lives. We begin to have the eyes to see it and the ears to hear it at the ebb tide of our community's life cycle. Rob is fond of saying that "what we focus on becomes our reality." If we begin to focus freshly on what's working, and on emerging signs of new life we may well experience the coming new life of God's ever emerging Kingdom. For many of us today, this is a far more satisfying exercise then focusing on what's not working and shaking our heads in despair.

The initial impulse to redevelop by beginning again inevitably comes when the pinch is felt between the beginning failure of present structures and the intuitive dawning of God's new movement in history. The coming awareness in consciousness of a new dawning is what feeds our motivation to begin again.

The new awareness is an acknowledgement of the failure of the past, as well as an openness to the future of God's healing Grace to overcome that past with the empowering Grace of new promise. The journey is refreshed (as we said in section one) with tears. Awareness leads to acknowledgement; acknowledgement leads to the courage to admit failure and ask for forgiveness; and asking leads to the acceptance of God's invitation to move on into the adventure of a new future.

In the larger picture of great historical cycles, we are at the Advent time of a new age. We are all being invited to be heralds and midwives of this new time by consciously building spiritual hearths within ourselves and within the villages of God that we inhabit.

Three Encouragements for Beginning Again

(1) Joy: The Transformation of Motivation

"Those who sow in tears [will] reap with shouts of joy."
                                        —*Psalm 126:5*

"Let me hear joy and gladness; let the bones you have crushed rejoice."
                                        —*Psalm 51:8*

C. S. Lewis wrote of being "Surprised by Joy." For Lewis, Joy was both a person (the woman with whom he fell in love and married late in his life) as well as an experience of profound release and exhilaration. Joy cannot be sought; it just happens in the unexpected experience of being loved and falling in love. We hunger and yearn to be loved for who we truly are. That yearning can be tearful, crushing and desert-like. The loneliness that I experienced before meeting my wife was excruciating. Experiencing Ira's unexpected and seemingly unconditional love gave me a hint of the joy that comes in discovering the loving connection we all are destined to have with the Source of All Things.

W. Paul Jones speaks of this Joy—which he calls the *transformation of motivation*:

> "The Advent season distills this profound negative-positive tension in experiencing 'joy as yearning.' Spirituality begins as yearning, edged in anticipation. Jesus is this 'yearning-as-event,' so wrapped in hope it becomes an enfleshment of the divine promise that 'your pain will turn into joy.' 'No one will take your joy from you,' for Christ came that 'your joy may be complete (Jn. 16:20, 22, 24).

> "In attempting to understand this joyful yearning characterizing both Advent and Lent, we are brought head-on to a major dilemma of the contemporary church: the question of *motive*. We ask again the question 'Why should anyone want to become a Christian?'

> "Today…what mainline churches offer is *supplemental*, promising to add to the quality of life offered by society. New people are attracted into membership by such factors as friendliness, diversity of activities, social contacts, congenial friends, youth activities, liveliness of worship, personality of pastor, convenience of parking, and church location. The modern church justifies its existence through its ability to offer cultural, social and personal services that supplement what is available in one's immediate environment. As a result, the local church is reduced to being one institution among many…joy is nowhere in the picture.

"The present interest in spirituality may be a direct reaction to this [joy's] absence, for I sense in searchers the yearning for another type of motivation. The heart of what the gospel offers is an *intrinsic* way of being. Christian existence is not lived in order to get anything, or to supplement what we already have. Instead, it is a self-validating way of living, for its own sake, needing no justification but the sheer *delight* of it....

"The primal experiences on which life's meaning depends are *intrinsic*. Priceless is losing one's self in a Mozart concerto, breathing the ocean's salty restlessness, and being mesmerized by a V-formation of migrating birds. Such moments of joy are a *sacred uselessness*, desecrated by even the thought of utility.

"So it is with Christian living. At its heart is falling in love with God."[82]

So we begin to journey again because we are in love with God.

(2) Trust: the Courage to Live Faithfully

At one of our diocese's earlier Convention's, Bishop Steven Charleston interrupted his keynote address to us on Vision, and said,

> "*I believe wholeheartedly that the Spirit just touched me with a wing and said "Steven, tell them this before you leave this garden.*
>
> "Jesus trusted God. If you want to live into the vision of the Diocese of Eastern Michigan, the Gethsemane experience is calling you, not only to your own personal commitment, but to your trust in one another. Laity, trust your clergy. Clergy, trust your laity. Body of Christ, trust your vision. And Bishop Leidel, trust your people. Eastern Michigan is an experiment in a new understanding of trust as the core of Christian community. How strong you will be in whatever storms may come will be based on how well you learn to trust one another. If you have undercurrents of distrust or misapprehension, in the name of Jesus bring them forward and clear them up and move together as a community. And do not let these threads of trust become weakened between you, for on those threads you will rise or fall as a diocese."[83]

Vision and hope can only become operational when there is a pervasive and a contagious trust in the community of our faith.

Daring to trust one another and daring to trust God's Presence and Goodness in the midst of uncertainty and turmoil is the essential attitude for today's soul-journeyer. As joy is our motivator, so we must allow trust to be our way of being in the world—our way of believing and seeing ourselves in the world.

Trusting requires courage. Courage and encourage are related words. St. Paul encouragingly roots our trust in relationship:

> "Who will separate us from the love of Christ? Will hardship, or distress, or persecution, or famine, or nakedness, or peril, or sword?
>
> "I am convinced that neither death, nor life, nor angels, nor rulers, nor things present, nor things to come, nor powers, nor height, nor depth, nor anything else in all creation, will be able to separate us from the love of God in Christ Jesus our Lord."
>
> —Romans 8: 35, 37-39

Believing, envisioning and knowing ourselves to be in the Presence of God's "loving arms" and keeping ourselves vulnerable to trusting relationships with others creates an environment where we can be who God calls us to be; an environment where confrontation and conflict are recognized as opportunities for revelation and growth; an environment where healing and transformation are unfailingly present.

Trust is a virtue that blends courage, faith, hope and presence. Paul Jones interweaves these attitudes in a helpful and convincing way:

> "The Letter to the Hebrews defines faith as 'the assurance of things hoped for, the conviction of things not seen' (Heb. 11:1). Conviction concerning things not seen is always in the face of things seen, often tragically. 'The sufferings of this present time,' Paul insists, reflect a 'creation…subjected to futility,' rendering faith a matter of clinging 'with eager longing' to an unseen hope that everything might be 'set free from its bondage to decay.' We 'groan inwardly while we wait' because only through a hope 'we do not see' that we are 'saved (Rom. 8:18-25). Faith is the courage to live 'with patience,' staring unflinchingly at a destiny in which 'for your sake we are killed all day long; we are accounted as sheep to be slaughtered' (Rom. 8:36)….
>
> "Permanence is an illusion….
>
> "To be finite is to dangle each moment over the abyss of nothingness, the 'primitive terror….' We attempt escape by projecting our anxiety onto persons and groups that can be 'legitimately' subjugated or destroyed. Ethnics, gays, women, and currently, 'terrorists,' are favorite scapegoats. Our minds are ongoing factories of idol making, but our escape is never permanent. There is always some nation, corporation,

party group, neighbor, or referee to trigger our primal insecurity. When our idols fail, we project the blame inwardly, into neurosis, an aversion to one's self. On and on goes the vicious cycle.

"**This is why [the] courage [to trust] is the only resolution of our primal predicament: it involves 'the road less traveled...'**

"Courage can be awakened only by confessing that the human dilemma is rooted neither in others nor ourselves. It is woven into the very fabric of existence. **This is why *faith [or trusting] is the only adequate expression of courage.* Faith resists self-deception sufficiently for us to live in the full face of life's tragedies. Christian courage means that 'we are afflicted in every way, but not crushed; perplexed, but not driven to despair; persecuted, but not forsaken; struck down, but not destroyed; always carrying in the body the death of Jesus...' (2 Cor. 4:7-1).

"Faith is the courage to act as if we are not cosmically alone....

"At this point we stand before the primal miracle of Christianity. Faith as courage without decisive evidence, trusting without certainty, can be none other then *divine gift....* Such courage is based on absurdities: accepting as kin those who would abandon you, showing compassion to those who intend your demise, forgiving those who intentionally abuse you, and loving a cosmos bathed in indifference. *Pure faith is living 'as if' with a courage that is 'in spite of.'*"[84]

Joy (the motivator for our journey) comes as we fall in love with God. Trust (an attitude of believing and seeing oneself in the world) comes as we courageously risk belief in God's faithful presence with us.

(3) Paying Attention:
Taking Time to Stop, Listen and Be with God

Ever since I can remember, my father has taken time to stop, listen and be with God. He has been a good teacher to all who know him. As a youngster I occasionally caught a glimpse of Dad knelling beside his bed saying his prayers. He stashed a copy of the *Day by Day* meditation booklet in the bathroom. One could not fail to notice the page that was unfailingly turned every day. I love and respect my father. I know and experience the prayers that Dad offers for me every day. So, I learned the habit of taking time daily to stop, listen and be with God.

Any significant relationship requires regular and focused attention to remain healthy, alive and growing. Saying "I love you" to my wife and taking time to pay attention to her by spending time with her keeps alive the reality of our affection for, and joy in, one another. As we are very different personalities, we approach the way we maintain our relationship differently. Ira has a gift for being able to give attention spontaneously and immediately as she sees the opportunity. I am awed at her ability to be so quickly available to me and others as needs arise. In contrast my attention to Ira can be very generous and extensive, but it usually comes in gulps that are interspersed with attention to other demands. Ira excels at multi-tasking; I am gifted in being able to focus intensely on one thing. Hence we are often challenged to compromise the ways we give attention to one another. Similarly our prayer styles are quite different. I am fed in periods of long silence and concentrated reflection and mediation; Ira is fed by being spontaneously present to people's needs and to connecting to the earth through gardening, and to beauty through her painting.

There is no one way or one technique or one set of habits that best enable us to stay open to God's love for us and God's presence to us. As we have discussed there are different gateways to God that work differently for different soul types. What we all have in common is the need to be intentional about how and when we pay attention to God.

Author and teacher John Ackerman offers a starting model for being present to God that he calls the "Stop, Look and Listen" model.[85] The model is reproduced in this guide as Appendix D.

It has been my joy to write this guide. I pray that it has been of some value to awakening your spiritual adventure.

> If you would care to be in contact with me regarding anything that I have shared, I can be reached at ed@leidel.us.

Just as I was finishing this writing I received in the post a gift of a book of poetry from a friend. The poems are of R. S. Thomas—an Anglican pastor who served five rural Welsh parishes before his death in 2000. I was especially attracted to one of the poems which will serve well as an ending to this work.[86]

Destinations

Travelling towards the light
we were waylaid by darkness;
a formless company detained us,
saying everything, meaning nothing.

It is a conspiracy, I said, of great age,
in revolt
against reason, against all
that would be ethereal in us.

We looked at one another.
Was it the silence of agreement,
or the vacuum between two minds
not in contact? There is an ingredient
in thought that is its own
hindrance. Had we come all that way
to detect it? The voices combined,
urging us to put our trust

in the bone's wisdom. Remember,
they charged us, the future
for which you are bound is where
you began. Was there a counter

command? I listened as to
a tideless sea on a remote
star, and knew our direction
was elsewhere; to the light, yes,
but not such as minerals
deploy; to the brightness over
an interior horizon, which is science
transfiguring itself in love's mirror.

Appendix A
Resources for Beginning &
Continuing the Journey

I. Recommended "Beginning" Books on Celtic Christianity and Spirituality:
    a. Listening to the Heartbeat of God: A Celtic Spirituality, by Philip Newell, (London, SPCK, 1997)
    b. Anam Cara: A Book of Celtic Wisdom, by John O'Donohue (New York, Cliff Street Books, 1998)
    c. How the Irish Saved Civilization, by Thomas Cahill (London, Sceptre, 1995)

II. Recommended "Continuing" Books on Celtic Christianity and Spirituality
    a. A Celtic Model of Ministry: The Reawakening of Community Spirituality, by Jerry C. Doherty (Liturgical Press, Collegeville, MN, 2003)
    b. Colonies of Heaven: Celtic Model's for Today's Church, by Ian Bradley (London, Darton, Longman & Todd, 2000)
    c. Celtic Light: A Tradition Rediscovered, by Esther DeWaal (London, Fount, 1997)
    d. Walking the Edges: Living in the Presence of God, by David Adam (London, SPCK, 2003)

III. Recommended "Beginning" Books on Christian Spirituality
    a. The Spiritual Life, by Evelyn Underhill (London, Mowbray, 1937)
    b. Spiritual Life: The Foundation for Preaching and Teaching, by John Westerhoff (Louisville, Westminster Press, 1994)
    c. Soul Making: The Desert Way of Spirit, by Alan Jones (London, SCM Press, 1986)

IV. **Recommended "Continuing" Books on Christian Spirituality**

    a. Listening to God: Spiritual Formation in Congregations, by John Ackermann (Bethesda, Alban Institute, 2001)

    b. Orthodox Spirituality: An Outline of the Orthodox Ascetical and Mystical Tradition, by an anonymous monk of the Eastern Church (Crestwood, St. Vladimir's Seminary Press, 1978)

    c. At Home in the Cosmos, by David Toolman, (Maryknoll, Orbis Books, 2001)

    d. …and any of the other books referred to in the **End Notes**

V. **Continuing Education and Conferences**

    a. *Listening to God: Spiritual Formation for Congregational Leadership*…a ten-day, two year certificate program offered by the Christos Center in Lino Lakes, MN. See www.christocenter.org/programs/congleaders.html or call (651) 653-8207

    b. www.rejesus.co.uk/spirituality

    c. *Convocation Workshops and Retreats*, offered by the Bishop and others— Dates and times to be announced

Appendix B
Summary of Type Dynamic Theory

The following descriptions have proved helpful to those who being introduced for the first time to the MBTI personality theory:

1. Each of the four mental functions (S, N, T and F) is available to each of us, but in varying degrees depending on our individual type.

2. We all use each of these functions both in our outside (extraverted) life and in our inside (introverted) life.

3. The more we use a mental skill, the more conscious (controlled) we become of how we use it. The less we use a mental skill, the more its use remains unconscious (uncontrolled).

4. Using all four mental functions equally is <u>not</u> the ideal; rather the ideal is to use each function as it is appropriate to the demands of the situations we encounter in life.

5. This appropriate use is a goal of maturity, not a gift of youth.

6. There is a normal development of the four mental functions for each type. The most used function is the "dominant" function, and the least used is the "inferior" function. The inferior function is the skeletal structure on which the "shadow" is centered. The shadow is the organizing center of the personal unconscious in the same way that the ego is the organizing center of the conscious self. The inferior (4th, least used) function comes from the same polar pair as the dominant (1st, most used) function. The polar pairs are S and N, and T and F.

7. "Normal" development can be interpreted by societal influences from parents, peers, teachers, communities, bosses, churches, and so on. Each person's development is a consequence of the interaction between his/her own gifts ("nature") and the influence of others who either support or try to change our natural gifts and tendencies ("nurture").

8. Thus, whatever your dominant function is, you will probably not recognize yourselves with equal clarity in the descriptions that we will be describing later. Even though you share a common "window" of personality tendency with others in the same dominant function category, you have a unique history of development that is yours alone. You and those who share your dominant function will have come under various degrees of societal influence, some helpful and some not so helpful.

It is helpful to reflect on the significance of this theory both for your external, worldly effectiveness and for your internal, spiritual development. In Christian thought (and especially in Anglican theology) the external world of experience and the internal world of reflection are of equal value. The external and internal dimensions of our lives influence each other. People with rich and diverse experience in the outer world of people and things have much data to inform and challenge their inner reflective world of thought, value, and feeling. Likewise, internally rich people will make increasingly conscious, informed choices in their external lives, knowing their inner thoughts, values, and feelings. They will understand better the impact of their actions on others and will be less subject to erratic, unconscious behavior.

Jay Hanson & Ed Leidel, January 1994

Appendix C
Descriptions of Experiences in
the Eight Deserts

1. <u>The Desert of **NONSENSE**</u> (Gift of Faith, Vice of Gluttony)
   PATHS INTO THE DESERT
   Preconditions for triggering journeys into the NONSENSE desert:
   - fatigue and pressure from over commitment
   - physical exhaustion
   - attending to practical matters for an extended period of time
   - dealing with bureaucratic red tape
   - feeling the pain of those who are victims of others' extreme aggressiveness
   - working in an environment where important values are being violated

   INITIAL EXPERIENCES OF THE DESERT
   When we are in the NONSENSE desert, we are literally out of control, though we would never admit it at the time. Heaven help the person who points out that we are out of control. Later, when the experience has run its course we say that we were "besides ourselves" or "out of character." We may be embarrassed that it happened, especially if it was in public. When we are stressed the inferior function can be a primary source of a lack of confidence in our natural gifts, making us vulnerable to the influence of others and to our own irrational thoughts and feelings. We are more likely to have these experiences in our younger years, but they can occur at any time. They more likely to happen to us when we are tired, ill, under pressure, stressed-out or burned-out, or are influenced by drugs including alcohol. When we are "in the grip" of the inferior function we experience the following feelings:[87]
   - "a sense of feeling numb and frozen with no way out."
   - uncharacteristic emotionalism
   - brooding
   - unable to find pleasure in things one usually enjoys—a lose of enthusiasm and motivation
   - "I have tunnel vision and lose my sense of time."
   - focusing on a single fact

- becoming overly picky, getting upset about little things, becoming irritable and cranky
- escalating small irritations into major issues, getting finicky about unimportant things
- becoming fussy, crabby, short-tempered and rigid
- "I become intolerant of interruptions and people—the very thing I usually welcome."
- exaggerating minor physical symptoms into major apprehensions
- taking any fact and blowing it out of proportion
- "I cannot respond to another's conversation. I pace, the traffic is slow, the clock is loud, sounds I never noticed before are deafening and very slow. It's almost as though time is standing still."

AGONY IN THE DESERT

As you continue to become possessed by the NONSENSE desert you may ultimately encounter the following humiliations.

- You may physically collapse and/or sense that your body is becoming fatigued or ill.
- You make many faulty perceptions.
- You become paranoid about other's value of your performance.
- You become so obsessed and bogged down with facts and details that you withdraw from tasks.
- You become depressed about your inability to perform and creatively engage.
- You experience anxiety, worry excessively, and find it difficult to sleep.

DRAWING WATER FROM THE WELL OF GRACE

It is often while you are in the *desert* that you find a *well* to nurture you back to life and to carry you through. Grace is the experience of God's saving power in our lives. Grace can be neither earned or managed. It is the experience of benevolent liberation at an unexpected moment. It is mysterious and beyond our rational understanding. It is very real. Everyone experiences it, but not everyone is able to name it. The primary Christian story of crucifixion and resurrection enables us to name this central human experience and to identify with it. Grace in the NONSENSE desert is often experienced in the following ways:

- The sensual experience of a sound, a touch, a smell, a color, a taste. Especially music, poetry, the experience of nature (mountains, ocean, falling water, animals), or a hug.

- The acceptance of physical limitations. The realization that one's primary vocation in life has definite borders and boundaries. The realization that you don't have to do and be everything.
- The experience of being on retreat (away from the demands of job and family) can lead to flashes of inspiration and intuition.
- Trusting and valuing facts, details, tools, or machines that you do not understand.
- The acceptance of physical care, structure, or planning that comes to you as an unexpected gift.
- The sudden awareness of simplicity or practicality in what appeared to be highly complex or theoretical.
- The sudden and unexpected awareness and appreciation of your own concrete qualities.

2. <u>The Desert of **BOUNDARY-LESSNESS**</u> (Gift of Hope, Vice of Lust)
    PATHS INTO THE DESERT
    Preconditions for triggering journeys into the BOUNDARY-LESS desert:
    - dealing with details, especially in an unfamiliar environment
    - unexpected events that interrupt planned activities
    - too much extroverting
    - others' intolerance, criticism, or misunderstanding of new and innovative ideas
    - others' intolerance, criticism, or misunderstanding of me as a person

INITIAL EXPERIENCES OF THE DESERT

When we are in the BOUNDARY-LESS desert, we are literally out of control, though we would never admit it at the time. Heaven help the person who points out that we are out of control. Later, when the experience has run its course we say that we were "besides ourselves" or "out of character." We may be embarrassed that it happened, especially if it was in public. When we are stressed the inferior function can be a primary source of a lack of confidence in our natural gifts, making us vulnerable to the influence of others and to our own irrational thoughts and feelings. We are more likely to have these experiences in our younger years, but they can occur at any time. They are more likely to happen to us when we are tired, ill, under pressure, stressed-out or burned-out, or influenced by drugs including alcohol. When we are in the BOUNDARY-LESS desert we may experience the following things:[88]

- "I stew about what's going on. I can't sit still and am restless."
- "Suddenly its time to do that thing I thought about doing two months ago."
- "I organize or clean."
- "I start tripping over things and feel out of control in the external world."
- "I nit-pick about things. I bombard people verbally and obsess out loud."
- Overeating. Over "anything" that has to do with the senses (TV, music, snacks, sex, etc.).
- "I feel anxious, exposed, and childlike."
- "I am emotionally aroused and am terribly critical of others."
- Cynical about anything of which I have no outer control.
- An expectation that obstacles and problems will forever plague you.
- "I try obsessively to control every detail."
- "I focus on negative facts."

AGONY IN THE DESERT

As you continue to become possessed by BOUNDRY-LESS desert we may ultimately encounter the following humiliations.

- You overindulge in sensual pleasures that harm your body or your relationships to other people.
- You become convinced that the outer world of things or people is hostile and un-trustable.
- You develop an adversarial attitude toward the outer world and drive friends away.
- You become obsessively angry and bitter towards others and "life."
- Your field of operation narrows considerably. Your range of acknowledged possibilities becomes limited and idiosyncratic.

DRAWING WATER FROM THE WELL OF GRACE

It is often while we are in the *desert* that we find a *well* to nurture us back to life and to carry us through. Grace in the BOUNDRY-LESS desert is often experienced in the following ways:

- Reading an adventure novel or biography of a courageous person where great risks are being taken and daring deeds are being done.
- Pulling weeds, smelling flowers, admiring the flowers' colors.
- Suddenly becoming adaptable to the task of arranging many details. Suddenly getting control of a situation.
- A change of scene or activity. A walk in the woods. Seeing a movie.
- Spending time in a space where there is no possibility of external interruptions.
- Discovering the freedom of embracing more realistic goals.
- Hearing and receiving expressions of understanding, sympathy, and empathy.
- Reading or telling funny stories. Reading humorous literature. Enjoying cartoons.

3. <u>The Desert of **CONFUSED VISION**</u> (Gift of Courage, Vice of Pride)
    PATHS INTO THE DESERT
    Preconditions for triggering a journey into the CONFUSED VISION desert:
    *   spending lots of time with people who are excessively serious
    *   spending lots of time with people who continuously focus on future plans and goals
    *   over committing to things in the future
    *   operating within a confining structure
    *   being forced to do long range planning
    *   becoming pinned down by too many commitments

INITIAL EXPERIENCES OF THE DESERT
When we are in the grip of the CONFUSED VISION desert, we are literally out of control, though we would never admit it at the time. Heaven help the person who points out that we are out of control. Later, when the experience has run its course we say that we were "besides ourselves" or "out of character." We may be embarrassed that it happened, especially if it was in public. When we are stressed the inferior function can be a primary source of a lack of confidence in our natural gifts, making us vulnerable to the influence of others and to our own irrational thoughts and feelings. We are more likely to have these experiences in our younger years, but they can occur at any time. They are more likely to happen to us when we are tired, ill, under pressure, stressed-out or burned-out, or influenced by drugs including alcohol. When we are in the CONFUSED VISION desert we experience the following things:[89]
*   A feeling of being overwhelmed by inner possibilities
*   "I get into a spiral filled with frightening possibilities."
*   "I am horrified that I won't ever be where I want to be."
*   The thought of future change makes me feel lonely and gloomy and dreary."
*   A feeling of unreality and disconnection from others.
*   "I start reading between the lines and attributing malevolent motives to people."
*   One becomes vulnerable to magical promises and "hocus-pocus."
*   It becomes easy to believe in grandiose, cosmic "visions."
*   "I felt totally abandoned by God who had been my protector and guide throughout my life."
*   "I experienced flashbacks as clear as videos."
*   "I was suddenly overwhelmed with anxiety, convinced that was carrying on an affair."
*   Worrying about irrational or imagined dangers.
*   Wild suspicions arise.

AGONY IN THE DESERT

As we continue to become possessed by the "grip" of the CONFUSED VISION desert we may ultimately encounter the following humiliations.

- You experience so much internal confusion that you are no longer able to make decisive judgments.
- Your inappropriate attribution of meaning to events undermines the confidence that others have in your judgment.
- You have grandiose visions that make you look foolish to others.
- You feel like you have to escape your life situation which has begun to seem like a prison.
- You think that no one ever will take you seriously because you feel like you are just a big kid.

DRAWING WATER FROM THE WELL OF GRACE

It is often while we are in the *desert* that we find a *well* to nurture us back to life and to carry us through. Grace can be neither earned or managed. It is the experience of benevolent liberation at an unexpected moment. It is mysterious and beyond our rational understanding. It is very real. Everyone experiences it, but not everyone is able to name it. The primary Christian story of crucifixion and resurrection enables us to name this central human experience and to identify with it. In the CONFUSED VISION desert Grace is often experienced in the following ways:

- The experience of being with "happy" people.
- The authentic experience of extra-sensory perception or mysticism.
- A sudden loss of fear of future possibilities.
- A surprising appreciation for the unknown.
- A sudden awareness of your own intuition.
- Suddenly being freed from a superstitious compulsion.
- Physical exertion and exhilaration.
- A feeling of being liberated from a confining environment.

4. <u>The Desert of **INCOMPETENCE**</u> (Gift of Duty, Vice of Sloth)
    PATHS INTO THE DESERT
    Preconditions for triggering journeys into the desert of INCOMPETENCE:
    *   dealing with people whose approach denies facts and actualities
    *   experiencing deviations from the present order
    *   experiencing suggestions for future change
    *   the prospect of unknown, previously inexperienced activities and situations
    *   overdoing or overworking a job
    *   doing other people's assigned duties to get a job done

INITIAL EXPERIENCES OF THE DESERT
When we are "in the grip" of the desert of INCOMPETENCE, we are literally out of control, though we would never admit it at the time. Heaven help the person who points out that we are out of control. Later, when the experience has run its course we say that we were "besides ourselves" or "out of character." We may be embarrassed that it happened, especially if it was in public. When we are stressed the inferior function can be a primary source of a lack of confidence in our natural gifts, making us vulnerable to the influence of others and to our own irrational thoughts and feelings. We are more likely to have these experiences in our younger years, but they can occur at any time. They are more likely to happen to us when we are tired, ill, under pressure, stressed-out or burned-out, or influenced by drugs including alcohol. When we are in the desert of INCOMPETENCE we may experience the following things:[90]

*   We becomes aware of all the ambiguous, shadowy, sordid, dangerous possibilities lurking in the background.
*   "I experienced an increasing lack of focus, confusion, anxiety, and even panic."
*   "I had an urge to leave work in the middle of the day and go to a movie."
*   "I couldn't stop expressing my pessimism and was a real pain to one and all."
*   "I am given to very sarcastic humor, slashing and unpredictable explosions of cold, hard statements about here and now reality."
*   "I get stubborn and let loose a negative barrage covering all the bad consequences of what is being proposed."
*   You come up with off-the-wall, unrealistic positive possibilities when faced with unfamiliar situations.
*   "When my husband was late, I buried him, and then dug him up and divorced him."
*   "I was having an anxiety attack. I was in a panic, a negative spiral, and I remember telling myself, 'Stop! Don't think about anything.'"

AGONY IN THE DESERT

As we continue to become possessed by the desert of INCOMPETENCE we may ultimately encounter the following humiliations.

- You no longer value facts and details. Nothing is trustworthy anymore.
- You engage in surprisingly impulsive activity, taking foolish risks.
- You compulsively overwork and don't trust anyone else to do the job correctly.
- You become convinced that the worst possibilities are inevitable.
- You lose all hope.
- You close down completely and become paralyzed in inactivity.

DRAWING WATER FROM THE WELLS OF GRACE

It is often while we are in the *desert* that we find a *well* to nurture us back to life and to carry us through. Grace is the experience of God's saving power in our lives. Grace can be neither earned nor managed. It is the experience of benevolent liberation at an unexpected moment. It is mysterious and beyond our rational understanding. It is very real. Everyone experiences it, but not everyone is able to name it. The primary Christian story of crucifixion and resurrection enables us to name this central human experience and to identify with it. In the desert of INCOMPETENCE Grace is often experienced in the following ways:

- The experience of poetry, music and art can lead to a positive experience of your "other side" (shadow).
- Paying attention to your dreams.
- Reading fantasy fiction, watching science fiction movies, or entertaining yourself with idle speculations and daydreams.
- Listening to "guided imagery" with background music.
- An unanticipated broadened perspective.
- An unexpected clarification of values.
- An impromptu acceptance of diversity and flexibility in relationships.

5. <u>The Desert of **MEANINGLESSNESS**</u>[91] (Gift of Love, Vice of Jealousy)
PATHS INTO THE DESERT
We are more likely to be drawn into the desert when
- feeling misunderstood, not trusted, not taken seriously
- feeling pressured to conform to a norm we don't believe in
- almost any interpersonal conflict, especially if we feel personally attacked
- not being allowed to express our point of view fully

INITIAL EXPERIENCES OF THE DESERT
When we are in the grip of the desert of MEANINGLESSNESS, we are literally out of control, though we would never admit it at the time. Heaven help the person who points out that we are out of control. Later, when the experience has run its course we say that we were "beside ourselves," "out of character." We may be embarrassed that it happened, especially if it was in public. When we are stressed the inferior function can be a primary source of a lack of confidence in our natural gifts, making us vulnerable to the influence of others and to our own irrational thoughts and feelings. We are more likely to have these experiences in our younger years, but they can occur at any time. They are more likely to happen to us when we are tired, ill, under pressure, stressed-out or burned-out, or influenced by drugs including alcohol. When we are in the desert of MEANINGLESSNESS we may experience the following things:[92]
- Excessive criticism:
  "Dumping" on other people;
  sweeping condemnations of people.
  "I become cranky, judgmental and angry. I mistrust myself and others."
  Become physically tense, agitated, yell, grit our teeth;
  lay guilt trips on others (as normal extraverted energy diminishes, the criticism can turn inward);
  self-deprecation;
  guilty embarrassment at this unusual behavior;
  low self-worth, depression.
- Convoluted logic:
  "My thinking becomes rigid and I insist on solving problems alone, with none of my typical sharing;"
  make up stories to explain some upsetting event;
  categorical, all or none judgments, based on irrelevant data;
  "become rigid, perfectionist, critical. I want the world to go away."
- Compulsive search for truth:
  must find the absolute expert who has the final word (but never trust we have found the person);

buy all the self-help books looking for the answer to the perplexing problem; go through lengthy internal dialogue to explain what has happened; may join support groups in search of someone who knows the answer; become focused on the one thing we can't do, rather than all the things we can do.

AGONY IN THE DESERT

As we continue to become possessed by the desert of MEANINGLESSNESS we may ultimately encounter the following humiliations.

- We have tunnel vision. We are right and everyone else is wrong. Our self-talk is of how we will teach them to recognize that we are right. Our verbal expressions demean their point of view.
- We are humorless. In minor manifestations, we may get a glimpse of our own ridiculousness, but in major manifestations we see nothing funny at all about our own attitudes or behavior or words. Thus, it is very risky to tease someone in such a grip; as in, "You are just in the grip of your inferior function."
- We make categorical, black and white, all or nothing statements. There are no grays, no middle grounds.

DRAWING WATER FROM THE WELL OF GRACE

While the experiences themselves may be unpleasant, and later embarrassing, they are often the source of learning and growth. They are another kind of Gift from God. Peter looked back on his thrice denial and saw something which he had never seen. In the grip of his fear, he had tried to remain cool and calm, but inside he was churning. It converted and energized him more than any of the gradual growth lessons he had picked up from Jesus the teacher. When we are in the desert of MEANINGLESSNESS we may experience Grace in the following ways:

- Discovery of limits of harmony; e.g.,
  Peace and harmony can't always reign; pain can help people grow.
  Ability to let others grow without "smothering" them with caring protection.
- Trust own thinking;
  Come to know its limits and use it wisely, learning to trust others' judgments.
- Better adjustment to adversity:
  Realize there may not be a perfect answer;
  Able to ease-off when feeling attacked, not so likely to take it personally; less reason to fight back or become self-critical.

6. <u>The Desert of **TRUSTLESS-NESS**</u> (Gift of Empathy, Vice of Anger)
   PATHS INTO THE DESERT
   We introverted feelers can also be provoked by
   - public personal criticism
   - disdain for our strongly held values and feelings
   - insensitivity to our need for silence, privacy
   - sense that others are intruding on our space
   - feeling controlled by arbitrary conditions that limit personal freedom

   INITIAL EXPERIENCES OF THE DESERT
   When we are in the "grip" of the desert of TRUSTLESS-NESS, we are literally out of control, though we would never admit it at the time. Heaven help the person who points out that we are out of control. Later, when the experience has run its course we say that we were "beside ourselves," "out of character." We may be embarrassed that it happened, especially if it was in public. When we are stressed the inferior function can be a primary source of a lack of confidence in our natural gifts, making us vulnerable to the influence of others and to our own irrational thoughts and feelings. We are more likely to have these experiences in our younger years, but they can occur at any time. They are more likely to happen to us when we are tired, ill, under pressure, stressed-out or burned-out, or influenced by drugs including alcohol. When we are in the desert of TRUSTLESS-NESS we may experience the following things:[93]
   - Judgments of incompetence:
     In early phases, we imagine others are judging our competence by little mistakes we make;
     then we start noticing others who make those mistakes;
     then we notice it everywhere: drivers on the roads, incompetent bosses, corrupt politicians, insensitive clerks.
     "I'm nit-picky and see only what is in front of me."
     "When I'm tired...I remember some incredibly dumb thing I did...or someone else's incompetence that reflects on my own will set me off."
     In serious episode, can think we are totally incompetent at everything, and wonder about the competence of those who should have caught our mistakes.
   - Aggressive criticism:
     "My humor becomes biting and cynical;"
     adopt combative, lawyer-like tone of pretentious objectivity;
     make almost vicious attacks on those who fail to live up to our ethical standards;
     may culminate in severe self-criticism.

- Take precipitous action:
  normally reflective and slow to act, we now do things suddenly;
  often make little problems into big ones;
  try to get things organized;
  make lists and check things off, with some artificial priority;
  withdraw from relationships, leaving burned bridges.

AGONY IN THE DESERT

As we continue to become possessed by the desert of TRUSTLESSNESS we may ultimately encounter the following humiliations.

- We have tunnel vision. We are right and everyone else is wrong. Our self-talk is of how we will teach them to recognize that we are right. Our verbal expressions demean their point of view.
- We are humorless. In minor manifestations, we may get a glimpse of our own ridiculousness, but in major manifestations we see nothing funny at all about our own attitudes or behavior or words. Thus, it is very risky to tease someone in such a grip; as in, "You are just in the grip of your inferior function."
- We make categorical, black and white, all or nothing statements. There are no grays, no middle grounds.

DRAWING WATER FROM THE WELL OF GRACE

While the experiences themselves may be unpleasant, and later embarrassing, they are often the source of learning and growth. They are another kind of Gift from God. Peter looked back on his thrice denial and saw something which he had never seen. In the grip of his fear, he had tried to remain cool and calm, but inside he was churning. It converted and energized him more than any of the gradual growth lessons he had picked up from Jesus the teacher. When we are in the desert of TRUSTLESSNESS we may experience Grace in the following ways:

- Awareness of limits of understanding; acceptance of our competitiveness; learn to live with and use power better.
- Acknowledgment of our competence; able to see that no one is perfect; that partial solutions can help.
- Moderated idealism; have learned to narrow the gap between expectations and performance from both ends; increasingly set and make achievable goals; learned to forgive ourselves and others, without watering down our standards.

7. The Desert of **POWERLESSNESS** (Gift of Administration, Vice of Bitterness & Vainglory)

PATHS INTO THE DESERT.

We extraverted thinkers can also be provoked by

- someone's apparent disregard for one of our cherished values,
- someone accusing us of coldness or not caring,
- our own fear that we may have been harsh with someone,
- strong emotions expressed by those about whom we care deeply,

INITIAL EXPERIENCES OF THE DESERT

When we are "in the grip" of the desert of POWERLESSNESS, we are literally out of control, though we would never admit it at the time. Heaven help the person who points out that we are out of control. Later, when the experience has run its course we say that we were "beside ourselves," out of character." We may be embarrassed that it happened, especially if it was in public. When we are stressed the inferior function can be a primary source of a lack of confidence in our natural gifts, making us vulnerable to the influence of others and to our own irrational thoughts and feelings. We are more likely to have these experiences in our younger years, but they can occur at any time. They are more likely to happen to us when we are tired, ill, under pressure, stressed-out or burned-out, or influenced by drugs including alcohol. When we are in the desert of POWERLESSNESS we may experience the following things:[94]

- Hurt feelings.
  Criticism, which we otherwise would see as constructive, we now take personally, and lash back at the source.
  The absence of praise, which normally doesn't bother us, now seems a clue that someone doesn't like or appreciate us or our work.
  In situations that would normally call forth our competitive powers, we now feel victimized, manipulated.
  Accomplishments which normally give us satisfaction for having done our duty, now make us feel like unappreciated martyrs.
  The sudden memory of an occasion in which we were insensitive causes us pangs of guilt.
- Outbursts of emotion.
  Having controlled our feelings for some time, in order to organize and decide things at work, we suddenly dump all our anger on our family.
  For no apparent reason we suddenly break into tears, especially in private.
  Having lashed out at everyone's incompetence we suddenly change to tearful complaints that we are not understood or appreciated.
  Have difficulty with intimacy; with expressing feelings appropriately.

- Fear of feeling.
Fearing that we cannot adequately express our distress, joy, anger, sadness, we maintain an outer calm while fighting internally to keep from losing control or "going crazy."
For fear of hurting others with strong anger, we cover it with biting sarcasm or cynical disregard.
In severe cases we may be alarmed to find ourselves contemplating suicide.

AGONY IN THE DESERT!
As we continue to become possessed by the desert of POWERLESSNESS we may ultimately encounter the following humiliations.
- We have tunnel vision. We are right and everyone else is wrong. Our self-talk is of how we will teach them to recognize that we are right. Our verbal expressions demean their point of view.
- We are humorless. In minor manifestations, we may get a glimpse of our own ridiculousness, but in major manifestations we see nothing funny at all about our own attitudes or behavior or words. Thus, it is very risky to tease someone in such a grip; as in, "You are just in the grip of your inferior function."
- We make categorical, black and white, all or nothing statements. There are no grays, no middle grounds.

DRAWING WATER FROM THE WELL OF GRACE.
While the experiences themselves may be unpleasant, and later embarrassing, they are often the source of learning and growth. They are another kind of Gift from God. Peter looked back on his thrice denial and saw something which he had never seen. In the grip of his fear, he had tried to remain cool and calm, but inside he was churning. It converted and energized him more than any of the gradual growth lessons he had picked up from Jesus the teacher. When we are in the desert of POWERLESSNESS Grace is often experienced in the following ways:
- Discovery of our own limits; e.g.,
Because others respect our minds they would like to know our hearts; unless we share them we will not have collegial relationships, but will always be one-up.
Our intellectual skills cannot meet another's need for warmth, for touching, for acceptance of their incompetences;

- Acceptance of the irrational, uncontrollable elements of life.
  Not every situation can be mastered; some must be accepted, abided, or abandoned. There is a "time to weep."
  Others' "irrationality" becomes a symbol of our shared human mystery, rather than a sign of their incompetences.
- Discovery of our need for close companions and intimate relationships in order for our life to be whole.
  Family animosities can be healed by expressing feelings; leaving analysis behind.
  Death can be less frightening, knowing we have bridged a gap that has long frightened us. "Suddenly, I knew I should reach out, take her hand...tell her...the good things,...not knowing whether she heard or understood. When I stopped, she began to cry."

8. The Desert of **LONELINESS** (Gift of Planning, Vice of Covetousness)
    PATHS INTO THE DESERT.
    We introverted thinkers can also be provoked by:
    *   public personal criticism
    *   disdain for our strongly held values and feelings
    *   insensitivity to our need for silence, privacy
    *   sense that others are intruding on our space
    *   feeling controlled by arbitrary conditions that limit personal freedom

INITIAL EXPERIENCES OF THE DESERT
When we are "in the grip" of our least preferred (4th, inferior) function; in our case, extraverted feeling judgment, we are literally out of control, though we would never admit it at the time. Heaven help the person who points out that we are out of control. Later, when the experience has run its course we say that we were "beside ourselves," "out of character." We may be embarrassed that it happened, especially if it was in public. When we are stressed the inferior function can be a primary source of a lack of confidence in our natural gifts, making us vulnerable to the influence of others and to our own irrational thoughts and feelings. We are more likely to have these experiences in our younger years, but they can occur at any time. They are more likely to happen to us when we are tired, ill, under pressure, stressed-out or burned-out, or influenced by drugs including alcohol. When we are in the desert of LONLINESS we may experience the following things:[95]

*   initially by a kind of slowness, vagueness, distractibility replacing our normal intellectual acuity.
*   Logic emphasized to an extreme:
    get emotional about being logical;
    inability to let go of a problem, even if we can't solve it;
    inarticulateness replaces normal clarity of communication;
    forget things, misplace them;
    suddenly become disorganized, not accomplishing much.
*   hypersensitivity to relationships:
    over-interpret or misinterpret others' innocent comments or body language;
    feel discounted when others don't listen attentively;
    become convinced we are unloved and unlovable, feel distant from humanity;
    may have felt different from everyone else as a child, and are now revisited by those feelings.

- Emotionalism :
  become irritable, unable to hold back frustration, anger;
  may even break things or fight with people spontaneously;
  may feel increasing self-pity, sense of being neglected;
  may have sudden outbursts of tears or rage;
  "I deny to others that anything is wrong but all the while I feel like I am drowning inemotions."

AGONY IN THE DESERT!
As we continue to become possessed by the desert of LONLINESS we ultimately encounter the following humiliations.
- We have tunnel vision. We are right and everyone else is wrong. Our self-talk is of how we will teach them to recognize that we are right. Our verbal expressions demean their point of view.
- We are humorless. In minor manifestations, we may get a glimpse of our own ridiculousness, but in major manifestations we see nothing funny at all about our own attitudes or behavior or words. Thus, it is very risky to tease someone in such a grip; as in, "You are just in the grip of your inferior function."
- We make categorical, black and white, all or nothing statements. There are no grays, no middle grounds.

DRAWING WATER FROM THE WELL OF GRACE.
While the experiences themselves may be unpleasant, and later embarrassing, they are often the source of learning and growth. They are another kind of Gift from God. Peter looked back on his thrice denial and saw something which he had never seen. In the grip of his fear, he had tried to remain cool and calm, but inside he was churning. It converted and energized him more than any of the gradual growth lessons he had picked up from Jesus the teacher. When we are in the desert of LONLINESS Grace may be experienced in the following ways:
- Awareness of limits of logic:
  acceptance of the illogical in life;
  one of the "facts" is emotions, learn to study and manage them.
- Acknowledgment of our vulnerability:
  reduction in our hypersensitivity;
  see that when we regain our senses, others' comments were innocent; its only logical they weren't aiming at us.
- Ability to express depth of feeling:
  others feel we are more a part of the human race;
  we feel less "different."

Appendix D
Stop, Look, and Listen
A Way of Listening to God[96]

Stop: *Breathe out and in. (Or walk, listen to music, etc.)*
Pay attention to your breath. Let go, let the Spirit breathe into you.

Look: *At the past 24 hours and your reaction.*
What is there to thank God for?
What are you not grateful for?
What internal messages were going around in your head? Say I'm sorry about hurting someone else?
Hand over my internal messages that are self-punitive? Ask for others?
What is your heart's desire? What grace do you need?
What is missing? You want _____ so that _____.

Listen: *To the Word of God in scripture, spoken to you today.*
Read aloud.
What shimmers, stands out?
How does it address your longing? Pray briefly and in a heartfelt way.
Let yourself rest in the goodness of God. How might you receive the Word today?
Respond. Is there something to think? Do? Be?
Write a few notes to yourself so that you don't forget.

"Look" is a version of a daily *examen* or examination of conscience. "Listen" is a form of *lectio divina*, spiritual reading.

End Notes

1. Ray Simpson, *A Holy Island Prayer Book*, (Norwich, Canterbury Press, 2002), p. 96.

2. David Adam, *Walking the Edges: Living in the Presence of God*, (London, SPCK, 2003), pp. 67-69.

3. Richard Foster's, *Streams of Living Water* (Harper, San Francisco, 1998) brilliantly characterizes six traditions: the contemplative, the holiness, the charismatic, the social justice, the evangelical, and the incarnational traditions.

4. *The Confession of St. Patrick*, Translated from the Latin by Ludwig Bieler, Downloaded from the Internet at http://www.ccel.org/p/patrick/confession/confession.html

5. Underhill, Evelyn, *The Spiritual Life*, (London, Mowbray, 1937), pp. 20-21.

6. Allen Jones, *Soul Making: The Desert Way of Spirit*, (London, SCM Press, 1986) p. 95.

7. ibid, p. 96-97.

8. Ray Simpson, Op. cit., p. 50.

9. *Book of Common Prayer*, p. 267 f.

10. Fredrick Buechner, *Whistling in the Dark, An ABC Theologized*, (Harper & Row, 1988). p. 105.

11. Ibid., p. 119.

12. Jerry C. Doherty, *A Celtic Model of Ministry: The Reawakening of Community Spirituality* (The Liturgical Press, Collegeville, MN, 2003). pp. 1, 9.

13. Ibid., pp. 15, 16, 19, 21.

14. (1) Loving relationships, (2) Inspired worship, (3) Functional structures, (4) Holistic small groups, (5) Gift oriented ministry, (6) Empowered leadership, (7) Need oriented evangelism, (8) Passionate spirituality.

15. Schwarz, Christian, *Natural Church Development: A Guide to Eight Essential Qualities of Healthy Churches*, (Carol Stream, IL, Church Smart, 1986)

16. The primary focus of this sabbatical will be *to determine what my role as bishop should be to nurture passionate spirituality in my own life to enhance my own spiritual passion as well as to model it for others. This sabbatical is also*

designed to enable me to coach and encourage the clergy of the diocese to become more effective spiritual leaders; to coach and encourage convocation leaders at quarterly regional visitations; to coach and encourage local vestries and congregations in passionate spirituality at weekly weekend visitations; and finally (a publisher willing) to publish a work that will flesh out the role of a regional leader hoping to become a spiritual guide to her/his people.

17. Hill, Michael, *The Religious Order* (London, Heinemann Educational Books, 1973) p. vii.

18. Ladner, Gerhardt B., *The Idea of Reform* (Cambridge, Massachusetts, Harvard University Press, 1959) p. 342.

19. Ian Bradley, *Colonies of Heaven: Celtic Models for Today's Church*, (London, Darton, Longman and Todd, 2000) pp. 45-54.

20. Ibid. pp. 55-56.

21. Jerry Doherty, Op. cit., pp. 29, 31.

22. A David dam, Op. cit., pp. 47-49.

23. O'Donohue, John, *Anam Cara: A Book of Celtic Wisdom*, (New York, Cliff Street Books, 1998), p. 109.

24. Philip Newell, *Listening for the Heartbeat of God* (London, SPCK, 1997) p. 95.

25. C Robert ahill, *How the Irish Saved Civilization* (London, Sceptre, 1995) p. 148.

26. Peter Tremayne is a pseudonym for Peter Berresforde, a well-respected authority on the ancient Celts. He is the author of twenty books, including The *Dictionary of Celtic Mythology, The Celtic Dawn: A History of Pan Celticism,* and *The Druids*. Berresforde lives in London, England.

27. To date there are eleven novels in this series, which all take place in a short period after the 664 Council of Whitby. For more information see www.sisterfidelma.com

28. Ray Simpson, Op cit., pp. 73-4.

29. Underhill, Op. cit., Chapters two and three of this work deal with each of these dimensions of the spiritual life.

30. Adam, Op. cit., p. 66.

31. William Countryman, *The Poetic Imagination: An Anglican Spiritual Tradition,* (London, Darton, Longman & Todd, 1999) p. 91.

32. John O'Donohue, Op. cit., p. 107.

33. W John esterhoff, *Spiritual Life: The Foundation for Preaching and Teaching* (Louisville, Westminster Press, 1994) pp. 29f.

34. Urban T. Holmes in *A History of Christian Spirituality* (New York, Seabury Press, 1980); John Westerhoff in *Spiritual Life* (op. cit.); Corinne Ware in *Discover Your Spiritual Type* (Bethesda, Alban Institute, 1995); and John Ackermann in *Listening to God: Spiritual Formation in Congregations* (Bethesda, Alban Institute, 2001).

35. **The MBTI** (requires a licensed practitioner to administer, score and interpret), **The Keirsey Sorter** (Instrument is in the public domain and can be self administered and interpreted); **The Ware Sorter** (available through her book, *Discover Your Spiritual Type*,op. cit.—this is the easiest and quickest of the three instruments).

36. Reprinted from <u>Discover Your Spiritual Type: A Guide to Individual and Congregational Growth</u> by Corrine Ware with permission from the Alban Institute. Copyright © 1995, the Alban Institute, Inc. All rights reserved.

37. Westerhoff, Op. cit., p. 55.

38. Westerhoff, Op. cit., pp. 55-56.

39. Westerhoff, Op. cit., p. 57.

40. Westerhoff, Op. cit., p. 58.

41. O'Donohue, John, Op. cit., p. 106.

42. Michele Evenari, Leslie Shanon, and Naphtali Tadmor, *The Negev: The Challenge of a Desert* (Harvard UP, 1971), p. 9.

43. Athenasius, *The Life of Anthony* (New York: Paulist Press, 1978), p.75.

44. Gregory of Nyssa, *The Life of Moses* (New York: Paulist Press, 1978), p.95.

45. http://www.esoteric.msu.edu/VolumeII/MysticalTheology.html, (Chapter II), pp. 205-206

46. Matthew Fox, *Original Blessing*, (Santa Fe: Bear, 1983), p. 41.

47. *The Theologica Germanica of Martin Luther*, translated by Bengt Hoffman (New York: Paulist Press, 1980), p. 96.

48. Teresa Of Avila, *The Interior Castle* (Westminster, MD: The Newman Bookshop, 1945), p. 114.

49. Kieran Kavanaugh, *The Collections of St. John of the Cross*, (Washington D.C.: 1973), *The Accent of Mount Carmel*, Book II, Chapter III.

50. Ibid., Book I, p. 103.

51. William Law, *A Serious Call to a Devout and Holy Life* (London: J.M. Dent & Co., 1905), p. 256.

52. Simone Weil, *Gateway to God* (New York: Crossroad, 1982), pp. 60-1.

53. Thomas Merton, *The Seeds of Contemplation* (New York: A New Direction Book, 1961), p. 80.

54. Martin Luther King, *The Power to Love* (Philadelphia: Fortress Press, 1981), p. 154.

55. Robert Wild, "I Am In The Desert" *Studies in Formative Spirituality*, Volume I, Number 2, May 1980, pp. 207-212.

56. Bradley, Op. cit., pp. 92-93.

57. An anonymous monk of the Eastern Church, *Orthodox Spirituality: An Outline of the Orthodox Ascetical and Mystical Tradition*, (Crestwood, St. Vladimir's Seminary Press, 1978), p. 37

58. Ibid., p. 37.

59. Ibid., p 82.

60. Where ever brackets [] occur, I am simply adding my own editorial comment.

61. Toolan, David, *At Home in the Cosmos*, (Maryknoll, Orbis Books, 2001) pp. 210-214.

62. http://www.filmsite.org/twot.html

63. Toolan, Op. cit., p. 215.

64. Ibid., pp. 217-218.

65. Ibid. p. 218.

66. As recorded at the conclusion of Bradley, Op. cit.

67. Bradley, Op. cit., p 55.

68. Ackermann, John, *Listening to God: Spiritual Formation in Congregations* (Bethesda, Alban Institute, 2001), pp. 125-126.

69. Ray Simpson, *Soul Friendship: Celtic Insights into Spiritual Mentoring*, (London, Holder & Stoughton, 1999), pp. 14-15.

70. G Margaret Guenther, "Spiritual Direction and Clergy Wellness: Is this ancient tradition helpful for 21st century clergy?," (Interview by NNECA news officer Joan Beilstein in *LEAVEN*, Summer, 2002), pp. 3-6.

71. Simpson, Op. cit., p. 163-4.

72. Adam, pp. 70-71.

73. Bradley, Op. cit., p. 57.

74. Ibid., p. 235.

75. Ibid., pp. 26-7.

76. Ibid., p. 44.

77. Elie Wiesel, *Messages of God: Biblical Portraits and Legends* (New York: Random House, 1976) p. 32.

78. The Community of Aidan and Hilda, *Celtic Models for Modern Churches: 12 sessions for developing people friendly churches* (unpublished, 2004) p.2.
79. Arlin Routhage, *The Life Cycle in Congregations: A Process of Natural Creation and an Opportunity for New Creation* (New York: Congregational Development Services, Episcopal Church Center) pp. 3-14.
80. Jerry C. Doherty, *A Celtic Model of ministry: The Reawakening of Community Spirituality* (Collegeville, The Liturgical Press, 2003) pp. 127-8.
81. See Rob's webpage at www.
82. W. Paul Jones, *Facets of faith: Living the Dimensions of Christian Spirituality* (Cambridge: Cowley Publications, 2003) pp. 118-121.
83. Address delivered by The Rt. Rev. Steven Charleston on October 23, 1999 at St. John's Episcopal Church, Saginaw, Michigan.
84. Op. cit., W. Paul Jones, pp. 129-132.
85. Op. cit., John Ackerman, p. 137.
86. R. S. Thomas, *Poems,* selected by Anthony Thwaite (London: Phoenix Poetry, 2002) p. 113.
87. Descriptions are taken from Naomi L. Quenk, *Beside Ourselves*, (Palo Alto, CPP Books, 1993), pp. 195-200.
88. Ibid., pp. 161-169.
89. Ibid., pp. 144-152.
90. Ibid., pp. 178-187.
91. Whereas the first four desert descriptions were created by the author, these last four desert descriptions were initially created by Jay Hansen as we prepared for our first "Deserts and Wells" workshop.
92. Ibid., pp. 129-135.
93. Ibid., pp. 94-104.
94. Ibid., pp. 77-86.
95. Ibid., pp. 112-119.
96. Op. cit., John Ackerman, p. 137.

0-595-31627-1